WRITERS
EXPRESS

SkillsBook

Editing and Proofreading Practice

. . . a resource of student activities
to accompany the *Writers Express* handbook

WRITE SOURCE®

GREAT SOURCE EDUCATION GROUP
a Houghton Mifflin Company
Wilmington, Massachusetts

A Few Words About the *Writers Express SkillsBook*

Before you begin . . .

The *SkillsBook* provides you with opportunities to practice editing and proofreading skills presented in the *Writers Express* handbook. The handbook contains guidelines, examples, and models to help you complete your work in the *SkillsBook*.

Each *SkillsBook* activity includes a brief introduction to the topic and examples showing how to complete that activity. You will be directed to the page numbers in the handbook for additional information and examples. The "Proofreading Activities" focus on punctuation, the mechanics of writing, usage, and spelling. The "Sentence Activities" provide practice in sentence combining and in correcting common sentence problems. The "Language Activities" highlight each of the eight parts of speech.

The Next Step Most activities include a Next Step at the end of the exercise. The purpose of The Next Step is to provide ideas for follow-up work that will help you apply what you have learned in your own writing.

Authors: Pat Sebranek and Dave Kemper

Printed in the United States of America

International Standard Book Number: 0-669-47170-4 (student edition)

7 8 9 10 11 12 -DBH- 09 08 07 06 05

International Standard Book Number: 0-669-47171-2 (teacher's edition)

4 5 6 7 8 9 10 -DBH- 09 08 07 06 05

Table of Contents
Proofreading Activities

Marking Punctuation

Editing for Mechanics

Checking Your Spelling

Using the Right Word

Sentence Activities

Sentence Basics

Sentence Combining

Sentence Problems

Sentence Variety

Language Activities

Nouns

Pronouns

Verbs

Adjectives

Adverbs

Prepositions

Interjections

Conjunctions

Parts of Speech

Proofreading Activities

Every activity in this section includes sentences that need to be checked for punctuation, mechanics, or usage. Most of the activities also include helpful handbook references. In addition, the The Next Step, which is at the end of most activities, encourages follow-up practice of certain skills.

End Punctuation 1

Choosing the correct **end punctuation** is a basic step in punctuating your writing. There are three kinds of end punctuation: the period, the question mark, and the exclamation point. (See "Marking Punctuation," which starts on handbook page 377.)

Examples

Native Americans welcomed the Pilgrims. ◀

When was that? ◀

That was back in 1620! ◀

> **Directions** Put the correct end punctuation—a period, a question mark, or an exclamation point—in the sentences below. Capitalize the first letter of each sentence. The first sentence has been done for you.

1 Have you ever wondered who the very first Americans were?

2 Scientists say they came from Asia thousands of years ago. At that

3 time, land connected Asia to the part of North America that is now

4 Alaska. Imagine that people followed herds of animals across the

5 "land bridge" between Asia and America. They needed to use these

6 animals for food and clothing. It was much too cold to grow crops.

7 The first Americans slowly moved farther and farther south.

8 After thousands of years, people reached the tip of South America.

9 It may have taken thousands of years, but it's no wonder people

10 headed south. Just think of living in a cave in a place where it is

11 cold and snowy all the time.

2/50

3 sentences

The Next Step **Write a paragraph describing your coldest experience. In at least two places, try to use a word, a phrase, or a sentence that would require an exclamation point.**

I was playing hiden seek with my frinds. I hid in a refridger. It was so cold.

End Punctuation 2

This activity gives you practice using correct **end punctuation.** (Check handbook pages 377 and 387 if you need help with this activity.)

Examples

He wears a cape and a big "S."◄

Who is he?◄

He's Superman!◄

Directions	Put the correct end punctuation in the sentences below, and capitalize the first letter of each sentence. The first sentence has been done for you.

1   the first superhero, Superman, came on the scene in the

2   1930s. he was created by a writer and an artist, and their cartoon

3   Superman was no average Joe how fast was Superman he was

4   faster than a speeding bullet he was also strong enough to bend

5   steel with his bare hands he had many special powers because he

6   was from a planet called Krypton of course he always used his

7   powers to fight evil

8   Superman was so popular that he was in comic books and

9   newspapers and on radio and TV when World War II started,

10   Superman had millions of fans his creators had to decide

11   whether Superman would join the army what did they decide

12   well, Superman tried to join the army, but he failed his eye exam

13   how could that have happened his X-ray vision caused him to

14   read an eye chart in the next room, instead of the one he was

15   supposed to read

The Next Step **Write a brief story describing a problem Superman faces. Use the three kinds of end punctuation in your story. (*Hint:* You should be able to use two or three exclamation points.)**

_____

_____

_____

_____

_____

_____

_____

_____

_____

_____

_____

_____

6/15/19

Commas in a Series

Commas are used between words or phrases in a series. (See handbook page 379.)

Examples

In a Series of Words:
Sprinters tend to be fast, strong, and energetic.

In a Series of Phrases:
Talented runners sometimes receive colorful ribbons, fancy medals, or shiny trophies.

Directions In the paragraph below, add commas between items in a series. The first sentence has been done for you.

1   Jesse Owens, an African American track star of the 1930s,

2   was born in Alabama, attended college in Ohio, and won four gold

3   medals at the 1936 Olympics in Germany. Owens often faced

4   prejudice disappointment and unkindness in the United States. At

5   the 1936 Olympics, he won the 100-meter race, the 200-meter race,

6   and the broad jump. He was also on the winning 400-meter relay

7   team. Even so, the award for best American athlete of 1936 was

8   given to a white man who had won only one medal. Other

9   Americans admired, respected, and cheered Owens. During a

10   parade in his honor in New York City, someone threw a small

11   white bag into his car. It might have contained candy, confetti, or

12   cookies. When he opened the bag, he found $10,000 in cash!

Commas Between Independent Clauses

A **comma** may be used with a coordinating conjunction to join two independent clauses. Coordinating conjunctions are words such as *and, but,* or *so.* (See handbook page 380.)

Example

Comma and Coordinating Conjunction:
I know the words to "The Star-Spangled Banner," *but* I can't hit all the notes!

(*Note:* The comma is placed inside the quotation marks.)

| **Directions** | In the paragraph below, add commas between independent clauses joined by coordinating conjunctions. The first sentence has been done for you. |

1   Americans have been singing "The Star-Spangled Banner"

2   since the early 1800's but it didn't become the official national

3   anthem until 1931. On November 3, 1929, newspapers announced

4   that there was no official anthem so people began to think about

5   a national song. More than 5 million people wrote to ask Congress

6   to choose one but many of these people didn't want "The Star-

7   Spangled Banner." Some people didn't like the fact that the music

8   was written in England and the United States had fought against

9   England for freedom in 1776. "America" and a few other songs

10   received votes but "The Star-Spangled Banner" won the day.

Commas Between Items in Dates

Commas are used to separate items in dates. (See handbook page 379.)

Example

To Separate Items in Dates:
The first drive-in opened on June 6, 1933.

▲

Directions   In the sentences below, add commas to separate items in dates.

1. On January 21, 1954, the United States launched the first atomic-powered submarine, *Nautilus*.

2. The first meeting of the United Nations was held in London on January 10, 1946.

3. United States president William H. Harrison died on April 4, 1841, just one month after his inauguration.

4. John H. Glenn, Jr., became the first American to orbit the earth on February 20, 1962.

5. The Central Pacific and Union Pacific Railroads met in Promontory, Utah, on May 10, 1869, to form a transcontinental railroad.

6. Do you know that on September 9, 1850, California became the 31st state to join the Union?

7. On October 27 1920 KOKA in Philadelphia, Pennsylvania, became the first licensed radio station in the United States.

8. The Brazilian team made soccer history on July 22 1994 when they defeated Italy and won the World Cup for the fourth time.

9. My birth date is April 23 1992; what is yours?

10. On November 3 1998 voters in Minnesota elected former professional wrestler Jesse "The Body" Ventura as governor.

11. Senator John Glenn boarded the space shuttle *Discovery* on October 29 1998 for his first return to space since 1962.

12. What do you imagine you will be doing at 2:30 p.m. on June 10 2025?

The Next Step Write a news story announcing the unveiling of a new car. Use dates to tell when each of the car's special new features was first developed. Use commas correctly! (See pages 379-380 for help with your writing.)

_____

_____

_____

_____

_____

Commas to Set Off Phrases and Clauses

Here's another place where commas signal readers to pause: after a long phrase or clause that introduces the rest of the sentence. (Check out handbook page 381.)

Examples

After an Introductory Phrase:
At the end of the 1500s, the first pockets were added to clothing.

After an Introductory Clause:
Ten years after Thomas Adams began producing chewing gum in 1871, bubble gum was developed.

| **Directions** | In the following sentences, place a comma after the introductory phrase or clause. The first one has been done for you. |

1. Long before batteries or electricity, a Greek inventor made a clock that was powered by moving water.

2. Best known as an astronomer Galileo also was an inventor—he invented the thermometer.

3. About 7,500 years ago in Turkey people used a natural glass called *obsidian* for mirrors.

4. A year before Thomas Edison introduced his lightbulb a British inventor made one.

5. When one of the first movies was shown people fainted because they thought the train in the movie would run over them!

6. Although we don't think of it as such paper is an invention.

7. Invented in China in the year 105 paper is now used worldwide.

The Next Step **Try writing three sentences of your own that use introductory phrases or clauses. Share your sentences with a classmate. Who used the longest introductory phrase or clause?**

1. _____

_____

_____

_____

2. _____

_____

_____

_____

3. _____

_____

_____

_____

Commas and Appositives

As you know by now, commas are used in many different ways. This time, you're going to practice using commas to set off **appositives.** An appositive is a word or phrase that *renames* or *explains* the noun that comes before. (See handbook page 381.)

Example

Cooper Elementary, *my school,* has 250 students.

| **Directions** | Use commas to set off the appositives in the following sentences. The first sentence has been done for you. |

1. Mrs. Chang, our teacher, won an award.

2. The award a gift certificate was for being an excellent teacher.

3. Our principal Mrs. Greene presented the award.

4. Mrs. Chang the best teacher I've had yet deserved to win.

5. Alisha a girl in our class read a poem about Mrs. Chang.

6. Mrs. Chang's husband a math teacher was there.

7. The rest of us sang a song "You're the Best" for Mrs. Chang.

8. Bobby a talented composer wrote the song.

9. We all wrote stories favorite classroom memories to put in a booklet for our great teacher.

10. Tamara a computer whiz made a banner on her computer.

11. The banner a work of art said, "Way to go, Mrs. Chang!"

The Next Step **Write four sentences, each one saying something about a different person you know. Start each sentence with the person's name, add an appositive that tells something about the person, and then finish the sentence. Use commas correctly!**

1. _____

_____

_____

_____

2. _____

_____

_____

_____

3. _____

_____

_____

_____

4. _____

_____

_____

_____

Comma Review

This activity is a review of all the different ways in which you've learned to use commas. (Review handbook pages 379-381.)

Directions   **Add commas where they are needed in the following paragraph.**

1   If you sometimes feel like sleeping all winter you might like

2   to have a groundhog's life. Groundhogs also known as woodchucks

3   sleep for six months every year. Although Groundhog Day is

4   February 2 groundhogs rarely wake up before April! While a

5   groundhog hibernates its body temperature drops and its heart

6   rate slows down. Bears raccoons and skunks who at least wake

7   up for midwinter snacks don't sleep as deeply as groundhogs.

8   Insects reptiles and amphibians also hibernate but they don't sleep

9   as deeply as groundhogs either. Groundhogs some of the deepest

10   sleeping of all hibernating creatures are rarely seen in winter and

11   now you know why.

Directions Add commas to correctly punctuate the dates in the following sentences.

1. On July 20 1969 Neil Armstrong was the first person to walk on the moon.

2. On June 18 1983 Sally Ride became the first American woman to fly in space.

3. Lewis and Clark's famous journey began on May 14 1804 and ended on September 23 1806.

4. The Civil War began on April 12 1861.

5. Lincoln delivered his Gettysburg Address on November 19 1863.

6. General Robert E. Lee surrendered on April 9 1865 and the last Southern soldiers surrendered on May 26 1865.

7. The Declaration of Independence was approved on July 4 1776.

8. The United States entered World War II on December 8 1941 the day after Pearl Harbor was bombed.

9. Hawaii became the 50th state on August 21 1959.

10. Delaware became the first state on December 7 1787 followed by Pennsylvania, which became the second state on December 12 1787.

Commas and End Punctuation Review

This activity is a review of commas and end punctuation. (See "Marking Punctuation," which begins on handbook page 377.)

Directions **Add needed commas and end punctuation marks in the sentences below. Also capitalize the first letter of each new sentence. The first sentence has been done for you.**

1   In the early 1800s, only about half of the children in the

2   United States went to school. at that time, many people thought

3   that only boys should go to school so girls were usually not

4   allowed to attend

5   However, Sara Pierce started a school for girls and she taught

6   those girls grammar reading writing and history one of her

7   students was Harriet Beecher Stowe ms. Stowe later wrote a

8   famous novel called *Uncle Tom's Cabin* Mary Lyon founded the first

9   college to accept women and that college was called Mount Holyoke

10   College Emily Dickinson, another great writer, was a student there

11   one teacher became famous for writing books for both boys

12   and girls he wrote the first American dictionary and his name is

13   still on many dictionaries can you guess his name sure you can

14   his name is Noah Webster

Semicolons

Semicolons tell the reader to pause, or even stop, before reading the rest of the sentence. (Learn about semicolons on handbook page 381.)

Examples

Between Independent Clauses:
I have a cat; he's a blur of gray fur.
▲

To Separate a Series Containing Commas:
I need to buy cat food, cat toys, and litter; ◀
clean the cat box, hallway, and closet; and
give Fuzzball a brushing.
▲

Directions Each sentence below contains two independent clauses that are separated by a comma and a conjunction. Replace the comma and conjunction with a semicolon. The first sentence has been done for you.

1   Roy C. Sullivan was a park ranger; ~~yet~~ his life was more

2 exciting than you might think. He was struck by lightning seven

3 times, but he lived to tell about it. No one understood why

4 Sullivan kept getting hit by lightning, and it's amazing that he

5 kept working! Lightning "fired" several of his hats, and one time

6 it set fire to his hair.

Directions On your own paper, write a sentence using the set of phrases below. Use semicolons appropriately in your new sentence.

see the lions, tigers, and bears ■ eat hot dogs, ice cream, and cotton

candy ■ be home in time for supper

Colons 1

A **colon** can be used to introduce a list in a sentence. (See handbook page 382.)

Example

I am interested in the following mammals: whales, dolphins, and porpoises. ▲

| **Directions** | Add colons to introduce the lists in the sentences below. The first sentence has been done for you. |

1. Reptiles have the following things in common: they have backbones, most hatch their young from eggs, and they are cold-blooded.

2. The following are all reptiles turtles, alligators, and crocodiles.

3. Alligators and crocodiles have some things in common they have webbed feet, their eyes and nostrils are high on their heads, and they are able to open their mouths underwater without drowning.

4. There are two ways to identify alligators by their rounded snouts and by their teeth, which are seen even when their mouths are closed!

5. Here are the telltale signs of a crocodile a pointed snout and only two lower teeth sticking out when its mouth is closed.

6. The following are all amphibians salamanders, frogs, and toads.

The Next Step Write three sentences of your own about animals. Include a colon to introduce a list in each sentence.

1. _____

_____

_____

_____

2. _____

_____

_____

_____

3. _____

_____

_____

_____

Colons 2

A **colon** may also be used to introduce a quotation. (See handbook page 382.)

Example

Joan Lowery Nixon said this about writing: "The idea is just the beginning of the story."

Directions   **Add colons where they are needed in the four sentences below.**

1. On the subject of honesty, Mark Twain said this "Truth is stranger than fiction—to some people."

2. I thought of something Abraham Lincoln said "It's a good rule never to send a mouse to catch a skunk, or a polliwog to tackle a whale."

3. I was scared, and I remembered this line from *The Lion, the Witch, and the Wardrobe* "Peter did not feel very brave; indeed, he felt he was going to be sick."

4. In *The Adventures of Sherlock Holmes*, Holmes says this about life "My dear fellow, life is infinitely stranger than anything the mind of man could invent."

The Next Step **Now write three sentences of your own in which you use colons to introduce quotations. (Look them up in a book of quotations, or take them from one of your favorite books.)**

1. _____

_____

_____

_____

2. _____

_____

_____

_____

3. _____

_____

_____

_____

Dashes

A **dash** is used to show a sudden break or change in direction in a sentence. (See handbook page 384.)

Example

Sometimes Laura puts grape or cranberry juice—how weird—on her cereal.
▲   ▲

Directions	Add dashes where they are needed in the following sentences. The first one has been done for you.

1. My brothers read all the Goosebumps books—I love the name

Goosebumps—by R. L. Stine.

2. Christopher Pike maybe you have heard of him also writes scary

books.

3. I have to go to the dentist my least favorite thing to do after

school.

4. We walked all the way home imagine this wearing our costumes.

5. Gary said and I don't believe it that he finished his homework.

6. Sarah isn't coming I don't know why so don't wait for her.

7. What's that old song Amber was singing it about the bayou?

8. Ben he's so lucky is moving to Florida.

The Next Step **Write four sentences below that use dashes correctly. The sentences can tell a story, or each sentence can be about a different topic.**

1. _____

   _____

   _____

2. _____

   _____

   _____

3. _____

   _____

   _____

4. _____

   _____

   _____

Hyphens

Hyphens are explained on handbook page 383. The following two activities give you practice using them.

Examples

With Compound Adjectives:
My sister chews sugar-free gum.

Between Syllables:
She also likes to eat frozen orange juice con-centrate right from the can.

Directions | Put hyphens where they are needed in the sentences below. The first sentence has been done for you.

1. Mom puts big pieces of chocolate in her chocolate-chunk cookies.

2. The governor elect has a lot to learn about her new job.

3. My great grandfather was a well known doctor.

4. I once made a long distance call to Japan.

5. I have an eight year old cousin who looks like me.

Directions | Use hyphens to show how you could divide the following words at the end of a line. (Some words should not be divided.)

1. history _____his-to-ry_____

2. writing _____

3. item _____

4. revise _____

5. improving _____

6. contents _____

7. connection _____

8. microscope _____

9. anyone _____

10. doesn't _____

The Next Step **Write a description. Use as many two- or three-word adjectives as you can. Then share your writing with a classmate.**

_____

_____

_____

_____

_____

_____

_____

_____

_____

_____

_____

_____

_____

_____

Apostrophes 1

Apostrophes are sometimes used to show possession. Other times they are used to make contractions. (See handbook pages 384-385.)

Directions In the following paragraph, use apostrophes to make as many contractions as you can. The first one has been done for you.

1   Jessica ~~does not~~ _doesn't_ like to sit in class on warm spring days.

2   She would rather be out playing baseball with Juan and Jennifer.

3   They are all baseball nuts. They will spend all summer playing

4   baseball, I am sure. Jessica always says it is too nice to be inside, even

5   if it is raining. I like baseball, too, but I do not like to play in the rain.

6   On rainy days, I would rather play computer games.

Directions In this paragraph, add apostrophes where they are needed to form possessives. The first one has been done for you.

1   From the age of 11, Clara Barton's goal was to be a nurse. A

2   brothers illness showed her that she liked to help sick people. Later,

3   with her fathers permission, she went to help soldiers in the Civil War.

4   Often she stood by a doctors side as bullets whizzed by. At the wars

5   end, she joined the International Red Cross. Later Barton crossed the

6   Atlantic to help feed Russias starving people during a famine. Clara

7   Barton will always be remembered for her unselfish devotion to the

8   worlds people.

The Next Step **Use the possessive form of each of the following words in interesting or entertaining sentences. (See handbook page 385 for help.)**

1. handbook

_____

_____

_____

2. desk

_____

_____

_____

3. Mr. or Ms. _____ *(your principal's name)*

_____

_____

_____

4. _____ *(your name)*

_____

_____

_____

Apostrophes 2

Here's some advanced practice with apostrophes.
(To get ready, review handbook pages 384-385.)

Examples

To Show Possession:
Blaise Pascal's famous invention was
a calculator. ▲

To Form Some Plurals: ▼   ▼
It is an invention with +'s and −'s.

> **Directions**   Add apostrophes where they are needed in the following sentences.

1. The zippers inventor was a man named Whitcomb Judson.

2. Judsons idea was to use zippers to fasten boots.

3. But in 1918, the navy used Judsons invention to fasten flight suits.

4. It wasnt called a zipper until 26.

5. The name "zipper" stuck in peoples minds.

6. The submarines inventor was David Bushnell, an American.

7. He built the first sub, but he didnt ride in it!

8. He didnt know whether it would work.

9. The first subs mission was to attack a British ship in 1776.

10. The sub, called the *Turtle,* wasnt able to sink the ship.

11. Most people know about the Wright brothers invention, the airplane.

12. It took off in 1903, but the first helicopter didnt fly until 1907.

The Next Step **Review the inventions listed in the handbook timeline (pages 478-487). Write about one of these inventions in a paragraph. Use at least two possessives and two contractions. (Have a classmate check your work.)**

_____

_____

_____

_____

_____

_____

_____

_____

_____

_____

_____

_____

_____

_____

Quotation Marks 1

What do **quotation marks** mark? They mark the exact words a person speaks. They are also used to mark the titles of songs, poems, short stories, articles, and so on. (See handbook page 386.)

Example

"Hi," Angelo said. "Where are you going?"
▲ ▲   ▲   ▲

Directions Add quotation marks where they are needed in the following sentences. The first sentence has been done for you.

1. Ricardo said, "I'm going to the library. Do you want to come?"

2. No, I answered. But will you check out a book for me?

3. Sure, Ricardo said. What book do you want?

4. I asked him to bring me any book that included nature poems like Birdfoot's Grampa and Something Told the Wild Geese.

5. Here are some great poems by Joseph Bruchac, Ricardo said.

6. I told him I hadn't read any of Joseph Bruchac's poems yet, but I saw one called The Song of Small Things in my literature book.

7. Be sure to read it, Ric said. It's awesome!

8. I will, I said. If all the poems are about nature, I'll like them!

The Next Step **Re-create a conversation you and a friend have had about school, sports, books, or movies. Be sure to use quotation marks correctly.**

Quotation Marks 2

Quotation marks are used to set off dialogue. (See handbook page 386 and the student model "Montgomery Mews Mysteriously" on pages 210-211.)

Example ▼ "Soccer is my favorite sport," Maria said. ▼

Directions | Rewrite the dialogue below about a soccer game. Add quotation marks where they are needed. Also start a new paragraph each time a different person speaks.

Did you see the game yesterday? Rodrigo shouted as he jogged up the steps leading to the art room. Yeah, it was great! Maria shouted back. I didn't think we had a chance. I mean, two goals to zero with only two minutes—I know! Rodrigo interrupted. I switched the channel twice before I realized what was happening. What a rally! Now it's the semifinals against Brazil, whispered Maria as they headed for their seats in the front row.

_____

_____

_____

_____

_____

_____

_____

_____

_____

_____

Quotation Marks 3

Quotation marks are used to quote either written or spoken words in the same way as they are used to punctuate dialogue. (See handbook page 386.)

(See handbook page 386.)

Directions   **Below are some quotations from famous stories. Add quotation marks where they are needed. The first one has been done for you.**

1. In *A Christmas Carol,* Charles Dickens wrote, "Scrooge looked about him for the ghost, and saw it not."

2. Rip's story was soon told, for the whole 20 years had been to him but as one night, wrote Washington Irving in "Rip Van Winkle."

3. In *The Adventures of Huckleberry Finn*, Mark Twain wrote, We went to a clump of bushes, and Tom made everybody swear to keep the secret, and then showed them a hole in the hill, right in the thickest part of the bushes.

4. At last he heard along the road at the foot of the hill the clatter of a horse's galloping hoofs, wrote Stephen Crane in *The Red Badge of Courage.*

5. In "The Legend of Sleepy Hollow," Washington Irving wrote, The night grew darker and darker; the stars seemed to sink deeper in the sky, and driving clouds occasionally hid them from his sight.

The Next Step **Choose one of your favorite books or stories. Write a paragraph in which you quote at least one sentence from the book or story. Be sure to punctuate the quotation correctly!**

Punctuating Dialogue

Written dialogue follows definite rules for using quotation marks, commas, end marks, and capital letters. (See handbook pages 215 and 386.)

Example

"Hey, Craig!" yelled Bill. "Wait for me!"

Directions Write in any missing punctuation in the following dialogue. Also correct any errors in capitalization.

1 Hi, Bill I said. Did you buy any new baseball cards at the

2 store

3 Yes, I did Bill answered with a smile. I had enough money

4 to buy 10 packs.

5 Great did you open the packs yet

6 No do you want to help me?

7 Sure! I hope you get some doubles I said. I will buy them

8 from you.

9 Maybe we could trade Bill answered.

10 Let's open the packs and see what you got first

11 Okay, and you think about which of your cards you'd like

12 to trade

The Next Step **Copy a portion of dialogue from a book, but remove all of the end marks, commas, quotation marks, and beginning capital letters. Then trade papers with a classmate. Correct the punctuation and capitalization in the dialogue you receive, and compare it to the original to see how well you did.**

_____

_____

_____

_____

_____

_____

_____

_____

_____

_____

_____

_____

_____

_____

Punctuating Titles

When you include a title in your writing, how do you punctuate it? The general rule is that titles of complete works (such as books) are italicized or underlined, while titles of parts of works (such as book chapters) are put in quotation marks.

Handbook page 386 explains which titles need quotation marks. Page 388 explains which titles should be italicized.

Examples

My favorite chapter in <u>Writers Express</u> is "Writing Poems."

"Too Many Cats!" is a story in a book called <u>Cat Tales</u>.

Directions	In the following sentences, put quotation marks around the titles that need them, and underline titles that should be in italic type.

1. The Lion King and Aladdin are movies with great songs.

2. Our science book has chapters called The Planets and Beyond and Rivers and Seas.

3. Part of a poem called The New Colossus by Emma Lazarus is written on the Statue of Liberty.

4. Little Richard sings Old MacDonald on his kids' album called Shake It All About.

5. Mom likes to watch The Simpsons.

6. My dad reads two newspapers, the Atlanta Constitution and the Wall Street Journal, plus Time magazine.

The Next Step **Write five sentences, each one including one of the following titles: your favorite song, CD, TV show, movie, and book. Punctuate the titles correctly.**

1. (song)

_____

_____

2. (CD)

_____

_____

3. (TV show)

_____

_____

4. (movie)

_____

_____

5. (book)

_____

_____

Italics and Parentheses

Italics and **parentheses** are explained on handbook pages 387-388. This activity gives you some practice using these special punctuation marks.

Example

Louisa May Alcott wrote a book about her family (it's called <u>Little Women</u>) and became a favorite author of young readers.

Directions   In the following sentences, underline all titles that should be in italics, and add parentheses where they are needed.

1. Washington Irving wrote a book of stories called The Sketch Book. Rip Van Winkle he's the guy who slept for 20 years is a character in one of Irving's stories.

2. Phillis Wheatley was a slave she was brought to America when she was about seven and never went to school. But she wrote poetry that was published in London Magazine.

3. James Fenimore Cooper he wrote both about the sea and about pioneer life met success with novels like The Last of the Mohicans, The Prairie, and The Deerslayer.

4. Early American writers created a new kind of story, the tall tale, about larger-than-life heroes Paul Bunyan and Pecos Bill are examples.

The Next Step **Write a sentence for each of the titles listed below. Use parentheses at least once in each sentence. Also make sure to underline words that should be in italics.**

1. <u>Writers Express</u> (book)

_____

_____

_____

2. <u>The Iron Giant</u> (movie)

_____

_____

_____

3. <u>Guinness Book of Records</u> (book)

_____

_____

_____

4. <u>Sports Illustrated for Kids</u> (magazine)

_____

_____

_____

Punctuation Review 1

This paragraph uses different kinds of punctuation you've practiced so far. Use "Marking Punctuation" on handbook pages 377-388 to help you.

Directions In the following paragraph, most of the punctuation marks are missing. First read the paragraph aloud, then correct it by adding commas, apostrophes, semicolons, hyphens, and end punctuation. The first sentence has been done for you.

1   The game of Monopoly is popular now, but it didn't start out

2   that way. Charles Darrow, the inventor, tried to sell the game to

3   Parker Brothers Company but they didnt want to buy it Parker

4   Brothers said Darrows game took too long to play, had mistakes

5   in the instructions and wouldnt sell Darrow had a few Monopoly

6   games made and he paid for them himself Monopoly became very

7   popular so Parker Brothers decided to buy it after all Monopoly

8   became the best selling game of all time in fact, more Monopoly

9   money than real money is printed every year How do you think

10   Charles Darrow would have felt about this

The Next Step **Write a paragraph about your favorite game. Explain why you like the game, why you are good at it, and so on. Trade paragraphs with a classmate when you are done. Carefully check each other's work for punctuation errors.**

Punctuation Review 2

Here's a challenge. This activity is a review of the kinds of punctuation you have studied.

Directions Some of the punctuation has been left out of the following story. First read the story aloud, then add the needed punctuation. (The number at the end of each line tells you how many punctuation marks you need to add to that line.)

1   Last spring, I visited my grandparents birthplace: (1)

2   Fredericksburg, Texas. There are lots of places to go in   (0)

3   Fredericksburg Enchanted Rock State Park Fort Martin Scott   (3)

4   museums and more. Another interesting place the Plaza of   (2)

5   the Presidents honors all the ex presidents who served in   (2)

6   World War II. But I want to tell you about a Fredericksburg   (0)

7   tradition—the Easter Fires It dates back to Native American   (1)

8   times.   (0)

9   White settlers most of the settlers around Fredericksburg   (1)

10 were German immigrants built Fredericksburg in an area   (1)

11 where Comanche Indians lived. One year, on the night before   (0)

12 Easter white and Comanche leaders were having a powwow   (1)

13 to decide whether to live in peace or to fight. Small   (0)

14 campfires dotted the hillsides around the town One pioneer   (1)

15   mother told her children Don't be afraid! The Easter rabbit   (2)

16   made the fires He is boiling your Easter eggs right now! Of   (2)

17   course, the campfires were Comanche fires the Comanches   (1)

18   were waiting they were waiting as anxiously as the   (1)

19   pioneers to hear if a peace treaty would be made.   (1)

20   Peace was made. The Meusebach-Comanche Treaty of   (0)

21   1847 is one of very few Native American treaties maybe the   (1)

22   only one never broken. The Easter Fires are still lit every   (1)

23   year and a play is performed to retell the dramatic story.   (1)

Capitalization 1

You already know that the first letter of a sentence is always capitalized. And you know that proper nouns are capitalized. This activity gives you practice with proper nouns. (For rules on capitalization, see handbook pages 389-392.)

Example

My family recently moved here from *Chicago*. (The name of a city is a proper noun.)

Directions **Find and change the words that should be capitalized. The first sentence has been done for you.**

1. Gustavo and I went with *D*dad to meet *G*governor *F*flood.

2. He came to our town to give a speech about mayor frost.

3. We live in ragener, south carolina.

4. The governor doesn't come here very often, dad says, but mayor frost is a friend of his.

5. So, he came from the capital city, columbia, to give a speech in honor of the mayor.

6. According to mom, governor flood would go all the way to mars for mayor frost.

7. According to dad, the governor would rather go to washington, d.c., than to mars.

8. He thinks governor flood wants to be president someday.

The Next Step Write a paragraph about a speech, game, concert, or other event you attended. (Or write about one you'd like to attend.) Include as much information as you can about when and where it was; any well-known people, teams, or performers you saw; and so on. Be sure to capitalize correctly.

Capitalization 2

Your handbook lists 14 rules for capitalization. That's a lot of rules to learn! In this activity, you'll need to use just a few of those rules. (See handbook pages 389-392.)

Examples

My father can speak *German*.

He is a member of the *Knights of Columbus*.

| **Directions** | Each sentence below contains several capitalization errors. Some words and phrases that *should* be capitalized are not; some words and phrases that *should not* be capitalized are. Make the needed corrections. The first sentence has been done for you. |

1. My Grandfather fought in the Korean war and in world war II.

2. In history class, we're studying the revolutionary war and the first President of the United States.

3. The league of nations was replaced by the united nations.

4. I've seen the California angels play Baseball in Anaheim Stadium.

5. The most common religion in japan is buddhism.

6. Our puerto rican neighbors speak spanish at home.

7. Most people prefer either coca-cola or pepsi soft drinks.

8. Jay got a McDonald's Hamburger and burger king fries.

9. Jonathan is jewish, and his family celebrates hanukkah.

10. Jamila, who is from kenya, knows how to speak swahili.

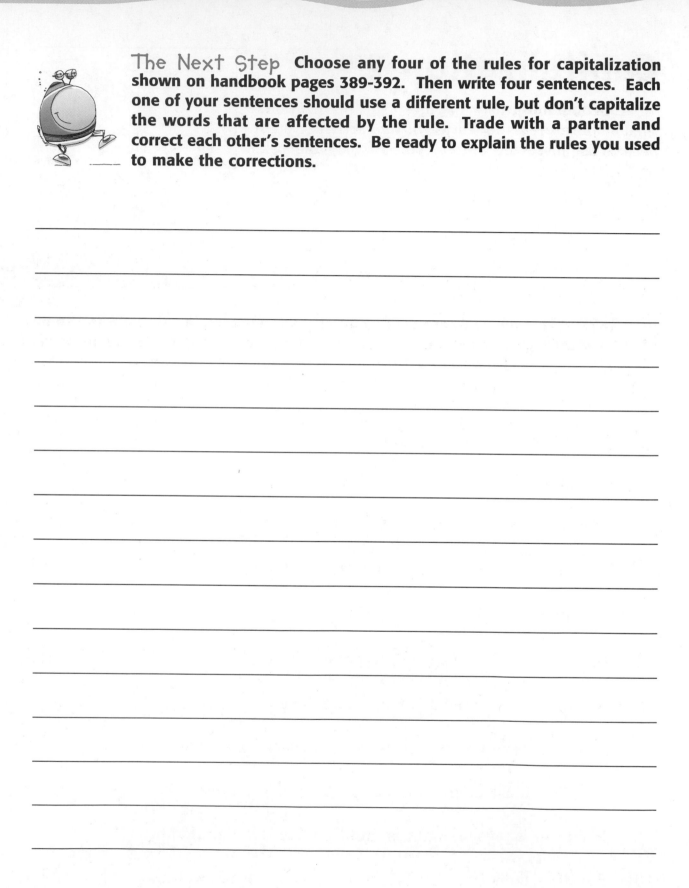

The Next Step **Choose any four of the rules for capitalization shown on handbook pages 389-392. Then write four sentences. Each one of your sentences should use a different rule, but don't capitalize the words that are affected by the rule. Trade with a partner and correct each other's sentences. Be ready to explain the rules you used to make the corrections.**

Abbreviations

An **abbreviation** is a shorter way to write a word or phrase—a shortcut! (Handbook pages 396-397 explain abbreviations and give examples.)

Examples

Dr. Bob is my dentist.
(Dr. = Doctor)

He is a D.D.S.
(D.D.S. = Doctor of Dental Surgery)

Directions Below are some abbreviations that are often used in writing addresses and times. Match each abbreviation to the word or phrase it stands for.

_____ **1.** St.

_____ **2.** Ave.

_____ **3.** Rd.

_____ **4.** a.m.

_____ **5.** p.m.

_____ **6.** Dr.

_____ **7.** S.

a. ante meridiem (before noon)

b. Drive

c. Street

d. South

e. post meridiem (after noon)

f. Avenue

g. Road

Directions Some other common abbreviations are listed below. Match each abbreviation to the word or phrase it stands for.

_____ **1.** lb.

_____ **2.** oz.

_____ **3.** etc.

_____ **4.** pd.

_____ **5.** M.D.

_____ **6.** Ms.

_____ **7.** Mrs.

a. Doctor of Medicine

b. pound

c. paid

d. ounce

e. Mistress

f. blend of Miss and Mrs.

g. et cetera (and so forth)

The Next Step Now choose any four of the abbreviations from the matching lists on the previous page and use them in sentences. (You may use more than one abbreviation in a sentence.)

_____

_____

_____

_____

_____

_____

_____

_____

_____

_____

_____

_____

_____

_____

Plurals 1

There are rules for making **plurals.** (See handbook pages 394-395.)

Examples

    pony ➜ ponies
    ash ➜ ashes
    class ➜ classes
    taco ➜ tacos

Directions   **Change each word into its plural form. Use the rules explained in your handbook.**

1. guess _____

2. potato _____

3. puppy _____

4. lunch _____

5. tomato _____

6. candy _____

7. bush _____

8. piano _____

9. key _____

10. box _____

The Next Step   **Now develop a "List Poem" using as many of the plural words above as possible. (See the model on handbook page 249.)**

_____

_____

_____

_____

_____

Plurals 2

This activity gives you more practice with plurals. (Use handbook pages 394-395 to help you.)

Examples

spoonful ➜ spoonfuls
half ➜ halves
justice of the peace ➜ justices of the peace
pulley ➜ pulleys

Directions   **Write the plural form of each word below.**

1. life _____

2. brother-in-law _____

3. stepmother _____

4. mouthful _____

5. roof _____

6. fly _____

7. radio _____

8. fox _____

9. mosquito _____

10. woman _____

11. wolf _____

12. sheep _____

The Next Step   **Write a silly paragraph using all the plurals above that name animals.**

_____

_____

_____

_____

Numbers 1

This activity gives you practice using **numbers** in your writing. See handbook page 393. It explains when to write numbers as numerals and when to write them as words.

Example

Twelve of us turned to chapter 5, but *four* students opened their books to page 5.

Directions In the sentences below, all the numbers are written as words. Some of them should be written as numerals. Using the rules on handbook page 393, find the numbers that should be written as numerals, and change them. The first one has been done for you.

1. There are ~~eleven~~ *11* parts in the school play.

2. We also need about ten people to sing in the chorus.

3. In the play, there are two children who are ten and fifteen years old; all the other characters are adults.

4. It takes only a few people to make costumes, and all thirty of us involved with the play will sell tickets.

5. If we sell tickets for two dollars and fifty cents each, we'll have to sell fifty tickets to pay for the costumes.

6. We could sell small bags of popcorn for seventy-five cents each, if two or three people would agree to sell them.

7. We plan to perform the play on February seven at either seven or eight p.m.

Numbers 2

This activity gives you more practice using numbers in sentences. (Review handbook page 393.)

Example

May *30* at *2:30* p.m., *five* teachers did a skit.

Directions In the sentences below, all the numbers are written as words. Correct the numbers that should be written as numerals. Then, on the line below each sentence, explain why you made the corrections you made. The first sentence has been done for you.

1. The population of our city is ~~one point three~~ *1.3* million.

   Decimals are written as numerals.

2. Our pie chart showed that only eight percent of our class had the flu.

   _____

3. Read chapters one and two, which include pages one through ten.

   _____

4. We voted sixteen to nine to get an aquarium.

   _____

5. We each brought four dollars to help pay for the aquarium, fish, and food.

   _____

6. My birthday party will be Saturday, May six, at two p.m.

   _____

Becoming a Better Speller

Making up sayings and acrostics can help you remember the spellings of difficult words. (See handbook page 307 for examples.)

Examples

Use familiar words:
conscience = con + science

Make up an acrostic (funny sentence):
through = **T**im **h**ad **r**ed, **o**range, **u**gly, **g**iant **h**ives.

> **Directions** Try writing sayings or acrostics for four words that give you trouble from the list beginning on handbook page 398. An example has been done for you.

1. _Their, there, and they're all begin with "the."_

2. _____

   _____

3. _____

   _____

4. _____

   _____

5. _____

   _____

The Next Step **Share your sayings and acrostics with your group. Choose the best examples of each and write them below. (You might also make a spelling poster displaying these best examples.)**

_____

_____

_____

_____

_____

_____

_____

_____

_____

_____

_____

_____

_____

Proofreading Practice

After revising your writing assignments, be sure to check for spelling errors. (See handbook pages 398 and 402-411.)

Directions | **In the following story, label the underlined words *C* for correct, or cross out the word and write the correct spelling above. The first one has been done for you.**

1   Last ~~Saterday~~ *Saturday*, we had an <u>advencher</u>. <u>After</u> lunch, we rode to

2   the woods to climb our <u>faverite</u> old maple tree. We had all

3   climbed the tree <u>befour</u>, but this time we <u>desided</u> to see who <u>coud</u>

4   climb the <u>highest</u>. Ron climbed even higher <u>than</u> I did, but it was

5   Rita who <u>one</u> this race. <u>Unforchunately</u>, she <u>coudn't</u> get down! She

6   didn't <u>realize</u> how high up in that tree she was, <u>untill</u> she looked

7   down. Then she panicked. She kept clinging to the branch she

8   was on even <u>tho</u> she was <u>geting</u> <u>tired</u>. Romero hustled as he <u>rode</u>

9   <u>straigt</u> back to his house. His dad called the fire <u>dipartment</u>. An

10 <u>enormus</u> fire engine, with an extension <u>latter</u> and with sirens

11 screaming, rushed <u>to</u> Rita's aid. Despite all the <u>exitement</u>, I think

12 we all learned a <u>lessun</u> that day!

Commonly Misspelled Words 1

Use the basic spelling rules found on handbook page 309 to spell words correctly.

Directions Following the basic spelling rules, add the suffix indicated to the following words.

	-able	-ment
1. advise	_____	_____
2. contain	_____	_____
3. treat	_____	_____
4. present	_____	_____
5. achieve	_____	_____

	-ing	-ful
1. care	_____	_____
2. shame	_____	_____
3. hope	_____	_____
4. play	_____	_____
5. help	_____	_____

Commonly Misspelled Words 2

You can avoid some spelling errors by learning a few basic spelling rules. (See handbook page 309.)

| **Directions** | Write the plural form of each of the following words in the space provided. |

1. thousand _____

2. Thursday _____

3. salary _____

4. anniversary _____

5. party _____

6. journey _____

7. toy _____

8. point _____

| **Directions** | Circle the correctly spelled word in each of the pairs below. |

1. their, thier

2. peice, piece

3. cheif, chief

4. friend, freind

5. weigh, wiegh

6. review, reveiw

7. relieve, releive

8. weird, wierd

9. receive, recieve

10. achieve, acheive

11. niether, neither

12. believe, beleive

13. nieghborhood, neighborhood

14. brief, breif

Homophones

Homophones are words that are pronounced the same but have different meanings and are spelled differently. (See handbook pages 402-411.)

Examples

dear, deer
rain, reign, rein
hair, hare

| **Directions** | In the sentences below, circle the correct homophone in each set of words. |

1. To ease the *(pain, pane)* of the burn, she *(blew, blue)* on her finger.

2. While on vacation in South Dakota, we hoped to *(find, fined)* a *(heard, herd)* of buffalo.

3. I would like a *(peace, piece)* of *(meat, meet)*, please.

4. My dad used a *(board, bored)* to row the boat because he couldn't find an *(oar, or, ore)*.

5. Once she realized she was driving the wrong *(way, weigh)*, she hit the *(brake, break)*.

6. The kitten licks its *(fir, fur)* with its *(coarse, course)* tongue.

7. He walked *(threw, through)* the metal detector before boarding the *(plain, plane)*.

8. The *(mail, male)* was *(passed, past)* through the slot in the door.

9. I'd like to *(buy, by)* a nice, cold drink, but I haven't got a *(cent, sent)*.

Homographs

Homographs are words that are spelled the same but have different meanings. (See handbook pages 402-411.)

Examples

   bear (1) a large mammal
             (2) to carry

   fast   (1) quick
             (2) to eat little or no food

Directions Use the following homographs in two sentences that show two different meanings of the words. The first one has been done for you.

1. blow   _Blow on your soup to cool it off._

The professional boxer dodged a blow to his right side.

2. row   _____

_____

3. last   _____

_____

4. might   _____

_____

5. racket   _____

_____

6. pen   _____

Spelling Review

Directions Look at the underlined words in the following story. Cross out the misspelled words and write the correct spellings above. If a word is spelled correctly, write C above it.

1   One September afternoon, we <u>quikly</u> changed into old <u>cloths</u>

2   and headed <u>too</u> our <u>freinds'</u> trout pond. Jutta and I <u>tackled</u> the

3   easy job—<u>neting</u> 10 trout from the holding tank for our supper.

4   Then Goetz used a rowboat to <u>pul</u> a huge fishnet <u>acrost</u> the

5   pond. Jutta kept the fish busy by tossing food <u>pellets</u> out in front

6   of the net. With Goetz on one side and Ron on the other, they

7   began <u>dragging</u> the net toward shore. <u>Their</u>, Jutta and I netted

8   the churning, thrashing fish. <u>Niether</u> of us <u>coud</u> believe it—150

9   trout! <u>Are</u> friends would have a freezer <u>ful</u> of fish for the winter.

10   <u>Finaly</u>, we moved all the fish into the large holding tank.

11   Meanwhile, Goetz's mother had finished cleaning the 10 trout and

12   <u>sesoning</u> them for the grill. By then we <u>wer</u> all getting <u>hungery</u>

13   and <u>impatent</u> for supper.

Using the Right Word 1

Your handbook lists many of the words that are commonly misused in writing. Use that section, pages 402-411, to help you complete this activity.

Example

accept *or* **except**

I'd **accept** the award, **except** I won't be there.

Directions Carefully read the following story. If an underlined word is incorrect, cross it out and write the correct word above it. If the underlined word is correct, leave it alone. (Work on this activity with a partner if your teacher allows it.) The first sentence has been done for you.

their

1   In 1849, the Riker family left ~~there~~ home in the East to start a

new

2   ~~knew~~ life in Oregon. Most pioneers traveled with other families

3   because <u>their</u> was safety in numbers. But Janette Riker, her <u>too</u>

4   brothers, and their father <u>choose</u> to make the trip alone.

5   One day, when they were in Montana, the men went hunting.

6   They never came back. Janette was left alone in the wilderness. She

7   <u>new</u> she would <u>dye</u> if she tried to cross the Rocky Mountains <u>by</u>

8   herself.

9   Since cold <u>whether</u> was coming, Janette built a hut and

10   chopped wood <u>four</u> making fires. She even killed an ox <u>so</u> she would

11   have some <u>meet</u>.

12   She <u>herd</u> wolves and mountain lions sniffing at the door at

13   <u>knight</u>. Can you imagine spending <u>weak</u> after <u>weak</u> alone in a tiny

14   hut, <u>weighting</u> for spring?

15   When winter had <u>past</u>, some Native Americans found Janette

16   and <u>lead</u> her to Oregon. They were surprised that she had lived <u>threw</u>

17   the winter!

The Next Step **Here's your chance to see how well you understand the word pairs you just studied. Use the following pairs correctly in sentences. The first one has been done for you.**

1. their, there

Their new car is parked over there.

2. new, knew

3. choose, chose

4. passed, past

5. led, lead

Using the Right Word 2

Many words are commonly misused in writing. See handbook pages 402-411. That section will help you to complete this activity.

Example

learn *or* **teach**

If I **learn** how to swim, Dad will **teach** me to dive.

Directions If an underlined word is incorrect, cross it out and write the correct word above it. If the underlined word is correct, write **C** above it. The first one has been done for you.

1 When settlers from Europe came <u>to</u> *(C)* America, they had <s>alot</s> *a lot* to learn.

2 There were <u>know</u> stores where they could <u>by</u> things. They had to <u>rays</u>

3 crops and hunt <u>for</u> food. Native Americans <u>new</u> all about the land and

4 the animals, <u>sew</u> they taught the settlers about <u>their</u> new country.

5 Did Native Americans <u>learn</u> the settlers to catch fish from the

6 rivers and <u>creaks</u>? Yes. They also told the settlers <u>its</u> a good idea to

7 put a small fish in the <u>whole</u> with the seeds when <u>your</u> planting corn.

8 It didn't make any sense <u>too</u> the settlers, but they tried it anyway.

9 It worked! The corn plants produced more ears of corn. The settlers

10 also <u>learned</u> to hunt <u>for</u> <u>dear</u> and other animals. They didn't <u>waste</u>

11 anything: they <u>eight</u> the meat and used the <u>fir</u> to make warm <u>close</u>.

12   America was full of things that the settlers had not <u>seen</u> or done

13 in the <u>passed</u>. They had never seen a <u>heard</u> of buffalo or <u>a</u> eagle or

14 eaten peanuts or cranberries. America <u>seamed</u> like a whole new world

15 to them.

The Next Step **Now test yourself by writing four sentences. Use the words listed below correctly in each sentence. The first one has been done for you.**

1. raise

The settlers learned to raise many new crops.

2. learn

_____

_____

3. creak

_____

_____

4. seam

_____

_____

5. heard

_____

_____

Using the Right Word 3

There are many words that are commonly misused in writing. See handbook pages 402-411 and use that section to help you complete this activity.

Example

set *or* **sit**

Set out the soda; then we'll **sit** and watch a movie.

Directions	If an underlined word is incorrect, cross it out and write the correct word above it. If it is correct, write C above it. The first two have been done for you.

1   *C*
     One week last summer, a boy named Billy went ~~four~~ *for* a vacation

2   with his ant. He had just scene a movie about sharks, so he asked his

3   ant, "Wood you go swimming with me?" Just as they swam buy the

4   deep-water markers, something whished passed their toes. Billy just

5   new it was a shark!

6   Billy yelled four help. His ant shouted, "It's a shark!" Alot of

7   people herd them, sew the lifeguard came to the rescue. He blue his

8   whistle and road a boat out to them. He told them knot to worry.

9   "We have some dolphins around hear who love too swim with people,"

10   he grinned.

The Next Step   **Write sentences in which you use each of the following words correctly. Exchange your sentences with a partner and check each other's work.**

1. past

_____

2. minors

_____

3. than

_____

4. their

_____

5. through

_____

6. waist

_____

7. choose

_____

8. scene

_____

Using the Right Word Review

This activity reviews some of the commonly misused words you have practiced.

Directions Choose the correct word in parentheses to fill in each blank in the sentences below. Be sure to capitalize the first word in a sentence. The first sentence has been done for you.

1. _____You're_____ going to get wet if you don't take _____your_____ umbrella.

   (your / you're)

2. _____ going to England to visit _____ uncle who lives _____ . *(their / there / they're)*

3. _____ time to give the bird _____ medicine. *(its / it's)*

4. He _____ what kind of cake he wants; now he has to _____ the frosting. *(choose / chose)*

5. Our teacher doesn't _____ late homework _____ when a student is sick. *(accept / except)*

6. _____ sister said _____ going shopping. *(your / you're)*

7. Cherie _____ she needed a _____ notebook for her project. *(knew / new)*

8. The _____ puppies were playing _____ close _____ the street. *(to / too / two)*

9. I don't _____ if my mom will say yes or _____ . *(know / no)*

10. There are so many _____ piled in our closet that we can't

_____ the door. *(close / clothes)*

11. Jeremy must _____ for the nurse to check his _____ .

(wait / weight)

12. If you make a _____ in your sleeve, you'll ruin your

_____ sweater. *(hole / whole)*

13. If I _____ to knit, I can _____ you how to make a

scarf. *(learn / teach)*

14. When the _____ splattered all over her, Carla thought she

would _____ of embarrassment. *(die / dye)*

15. I planned to write _____ letter, _____ editorial. *(a / an)*

The Next Step Write a sentence using each pair of words below correctly.

1. led, lead _____

_____

2. threw, through _____

_____

3. buy, by _____

_____

Sentence Activities

The activities in this section cover four important areas: (1) the basic parts, types, and kinds of sentences; (2) the methods for writing smooth-reading sentences; (3) common sentence errors; and (4) ways to add variety to sentences. Most activities contain a main practice part, in which you review, combine, or analyze sentences. In addition, The Next Step activities give you follow-up practice with certain skills.

Simple Subjects and Verbs

What are the basic parts that every sentence must have? If you answered a **subject** and a **verb,** you are right. (See pages 114 and 412-413 in your handbook.)

Examples

Fish swim in the ocean.

Birds fly in the sky.

| **Directions** | On handbook page 104, look at the model description of a place, "Camp Knollwood." The second paragraph has five sentences. Find the subject in each sentence. Then rewrite the sentences, changing the subject. The new subject can be anything you choose, as long as it makes a correct sentence. Circle your new subjects. The first two have been done for you as an example. |

1. _Over by the evergreens were many (squirrels.)_ _____

2. _The (hats) were small, blue, and floppy._ _____

3. _____

   _____

4. _____

   _____

5. _____

   _____

The Next Step **Now go back to the same five sentences in your handbook and rewrite them again. This time change the verb instead of the subject. Circle your new verbs.**

1. _____

_____

2. _____

_____

3. _____

_____

4. _____

_____

5. _____

_____

Compound Subjects and Predicates

A sentence may have more than one subject (called a **compound subject**) or more than one predicate (called a **compound predicate**). In fact, a sentence may even have both a compound subject and a compound predicate. (See handbook pages 412-413.)

Examples

Compound Subject: My <u>sister</u> and her <u>friend</u> <u>went</u> to a movie.

Compound Predicate: <u>They</u> <u>ate</u> popcorn and <u>drank</u> soda.

Directions   **Rewrite each of the following sentences two times. The first time, change the sentence so that it has a compound subject. The second time, change the sentence so that it has a compound predicate. The first one has been done for you.**

1. Tracy moved to Arizona.

Compound Subject: <u>Tracy and Teddi moved to Arizona.</u>

Compound Predicate: <u>Tracy moved to Arizona and started school.</u>

2. Tracy's grandmother lives there.

Compound Subject: _____

_____

Compound Predicate: _____

_____

3. Tracy wrote us a letter.

Compound Subject: _____

_____

Compound Predicate: _____

_____

4. Tracy goes swimming every day.

Compound Subject: _____

_____

Compound Predicate: _____

_____

The Next Step **Write one sentence that has a compound subject, one sentence that has a compound predicate, and one sentence that has both. Your sentences can be about Tracy and her family in Arizona, or about anything you like.**

1. *Compound Subject:* _____

_____

2. *Compound Predicate:* _____

_____

3. *Compound Subject and Compound Predicate:* _____

_____

_____

Prepositional Phrases

A **prepositional phrase** includes a preposition, the object of the preposition, and any describing words that come in between. (You'll find a list of prepositions on handbook page 434.)

Examples

He ran *through the doorway.*
(This prepositional phrase includes the preposition "through," the noun object "doorway," and the adjective "the.")
Without a doubt they had the flu.

Directions **Each sentence below has at least one prepositional phrase. (Six of the sentences have two prepositional phrases.) Circle each preposition, and underline each prepositional phrase. The first sentence has been done for you.**

1. David made a valentine (for) his mom.

2. It was in the shape of a heart.

3. It had a picture of flowers on the front.

4. David wrote a poem inside the card.

5. It was about all the things his mom does for him.

6. He signed his name beneath the poem.

7. Then he put the card in an envelope he made.

8. He gave it to his mom after school.

9. She told everyone about the card she got from David.

10. She took the card to work and put it on her desk.

| **Directions** | Write four more sentences about David's mom's valentine. For example, you could write about the people who saw it at her office, about what happened to the valentine next, and so on. Make sure to use at least one prepositional phrase in each of your sentences. Circle the prepositions and underline the prepositional phrases. |

1. _____

_____

_____

2. _____

_____

_____

3. _____

_____

_____

4. _____

_____

_____

Clauses

A **clause** is a group of related words that has both a subject and a predicate. An **independent clause** expresses a complete thought and can stand alone as a sentence. A **dependent clause** does not express a complete thought and cannot stand alone. (See handbook page 414.)

Examples

Independent Clause: Our old VCR worked

Dependent Clause: After we fixed the remote control

Directions On the line before each clause, write *D* if it is a dependent clause and *I* if it is an independent clause. Add correct end punctuation for each independent clause. The first one has been done for you.

_____I_____ **1.** We got a new VCR.

_____ **2.** When we lost the remote control

_____ **3.** After Max put his peanut butter sandwich in it

_____ **4.** Max is only three

_____ **5.** Since the sandwich was in there

_____ **6.** A million ants crawled into the VCR

_____ **7.** When my dad found out

_____ **8.** Until Max gets older

_____ **9.** The new VCR sits on a high shelf

_____ **10.** Where Max can't reach it

_____ **11.** Although Max broke the VCR

_____ **12.** Mom says Max is creative

Directions Make each dependent clause on the previous page into a complete sentence. To do this, add an independent clause. The first one has been done for you.

1. When we lost the remote control, we forgot how to start the VCR.

2. _____

   _____

3. _____

   _____

4. _____

   _____

5. _____

   _____

6. _____

   _____

7. _____

   _____

Simple, Compound, and Complex Sentences 1

Read about **simple**, **compound**, and **complex** sentences on handbook page 415. See the model simple sentences on page 415 and the compound and complex sentences on page 121.

Examples

    Simple Sentence: Charlotte is shy.

  Compound Sentence: She is quiet, but she can be daring.

    Complex Sentence: I like Charlotte because she is like me.

Directions	On the lines below, write *simple, compound,* or *complex* to identify each sentence. The hardest one has been done for you!

_____ **1.** *The True Confessions of Charlotte Doyle* is about a wealthy thirteen-year-old girl named Charlotte.

_____ **2.** In 1832, Charlotte is supposed to sail from England to Rhode Island with two other families, but the families never show up.

_____ **3.** Charlotte decides to sail with the crew alone.

_____ **4.** She remains good friends with the captain, until the captain kills two of the crewmen for being traitors.

_____ **5.** Charlotte then decides to join the crew and becomes "Mr. Doyle" in the logbook.

_____ **6.** During a storm, the first mate is killed with her knife!

complex **7.** Avi, the author, wanted to tell his readers that even shy people like Charlotte can become brave.

Simple, Compound, and Complex Sentences 2

Review the types of sentences on handbook page 415. (You may also read about clauses on page 414 and about compound and complex sentences on page 121.)

Examples

Compound Sentence: I have a 4-H cow, and she is a Black Angus.

Complex Sentence: I named her Swartzie because she's as black as coal.

| **Directions** | Rewrite the following simple sentences. First add an independent clause (another simple sentence) to make a compound sentence. Then add a dependent clause to make a complex sentence. |

1. Raul has new skates.

Compound: _____

Complex: _____

_____

2. Anya's school has a computer club.

Compound: _____

Complex: _____

_____

3. Dad cooks Italian food.

Compound: _____

Complex: _____

_____

Kinds of Sentences 1

There are four kinds of sentences: **declarative, interrogative, imperative,** and **exclamatory.** (See handbook page 416.)

Examples

Declarative Sentence:
The Sears Tower is a famous skyscraper.

Interrogative Sentence:
How many states can you see from the top of this building?

Imperative Sentence:
You must go to the top.

Exclamatory Sentence:
The people on the ground look like ants!

Directions   **Recall a time you had an awesome experience. Maybe you went to the top of a skyscraper, got stuck on the top of a Ferris wheel, or rode a dirt bike for the first time. Write one sentence of each kind about your experience.**

Declarative: _____

_____

Interrogative: _____

_____

Imperative: _____

_____

Exclamatory: _____

_____

Kinds of Sentences 2

This activity gives you some practice identifying the four kinds of sentences: **declarative, interrogative, imperative,** and **exclamatory.** (See handbook page 416.)

Directions   **In your handbook, find an example of each kind of sentence. Copy the sentences onto the chart. (Hint: Look for sentences in the "Story and Playwriting" section, which begins on page 208.)**

Declarative Sentence:
Interrogative Sentence:
Imperative Sentence:
Exclamatory Sentence:

Combining Sentences with Key Words

You can combine sentences by moving a **key word** from one sentence to another. (See handbook page 119.)

Example

Short Sentences: I lost my book.
                    It's my math book.

Combined Sentence: I lost my math book.

Directions   Combine each pair of sentences below by moving a key word from the second sentence into the first. Underline each key word you use. The first one has been done for you.

1. Our teacher found a kitten. It is <u>tiny</u>.

   Our teacher found a tiny kitten.
   _____

2. Our classroom computer crashed. It happened yesterday.

   _____

3. My dog snores. He snores loudly.

   _____

4. My friend Willy wrote a story. It's a fantasy.

   _____

5. We're going to the park. We're going there later.

   _____

The Next Step Fill in each blank below with any adjective or adverb that makes sense. Then combine each pair of sentences, using the word you filled in as a key word. The first one has been done for you.

1. Dinah opened the door. She opened it _____ *slowly* _____ .

Dinah opened the door slowly.

2. The door creaked. It creaked _____ .

_____

3. Aunt Millie was wearing a hat. The hat was _____ .

_____

4. Mason painted his room. He painted it _____ .

_____

5. Sarah was wearing a costume. The costume was _____ .

_____

6. The cat purred. It purred _____ .

_____

7. My mom grows roses. They are _____ .

_____

Combining Sentences with Phrases

You can combine sentences by moving a **phrase** from one sentence to another. (See handbook page 120.)

Example

Two Sentences: Just then the phone rang. The phone is in the hall.

Combined Sentence: Just then the phone in the hall rang.

| **Directions** | For each pair of sentences below, underline a phrase from the second sentence that you can move to the first sentence. Then combine the sentences. The first one has been done for you. |

1. Something scary happened last night. It happened <u>in our neighborhood</u>.

   Something scary happened last night in our neighborhood.

2. The lights went out. They went out at about 9:00.

   _____

3. Barney started barking like crazy. Barney is our dog.

   _____

4. I was watching TV until the TV went off. I was watching by myself.

   _____

5. I yelled, "Mom!" I yelled at the top of my lungs.

   _____

6. She got a flashlight. She took it out of the closet.

   _____

Directions Fill in the blanks to complete the following sentences any way you like. Then combine each pair of sentences. The first one has been done for you.

1. _____ *Linda* _____ went to the Monroe County Fair. She is my

   _____ *cousin* _____ .

   Linda, my cousin, went to the Monroe County Fair.

2. _____ loves chocolate. She is my _____ .

   _____

   _____

3. Mugs is sleeping. He is sleeping _____ .

   _____

   _____

4. I found a box of pennies. I found it _____ .

   _____

   _____

5. _____ took a trip. He went to _____ .

   _____

   _____

6. _____ has a horse. It is _____ .

   _____

   _____

Combining Sentences with a Series of Words or Phrases 1

You can combine short sentences using a **series of words** or **phrases.** (See handbook page 119.)

Example

Short Sentences: The winters here are too long. They are too cold. They are also too snowy.

Combined Sentence: The winters here are too long, too cold, and too snowy.

Directions Use a series of words or phrases to combine each group of sentences below. The first one has been done for you.

1. The river has steep banks. It has a fast current. It has dangerous falls.

   The river has steep banks, a fast current, and dangerous falls.

2. Last night we heard chirping crickets. We also heard hooting owls. We also heard howling coyotes.

   _____

   _____

3. Dad puts tomatoes in his spaghetti sauce. He also puts in mushrooms. He also puts in onions.

   _____

   _____

4. It was cool in the cave. It was dark. It was damp.

   _____

Directions Fill in the blanks below with any words or phrases that make sense. Then combine each group of sentences. The first one has been done for you.

1. Garter snakes are ___small___ . They are ___colorful___ .

   They are also ___harmless___ .

   Garter snakes are small, colorful, and harmless.

2. Elephants have _____ . They also have _____ .

   They also have _____ .

   _____

   _____

3. Ghosts are _____ . They are _____ .

   They are _____ .

   _____

   _____

4. Aliens from outer space have _____ .

   They also have _____ . They also have _____ .

   _____

   _____

Combining Sentences with a Series of Words or Phrases 2

Handbook pages 119 and 120 explain ways to combine sentences. Review those pages; then do this practice activity.

Example

Short Sentences: Jon got a baseball on his birthday. He got a T-shirt. He got a parrot.

Combined Sentence: Jon got a baseball, a T-shirt, and a parrot on his birthday.

Directions **Combine the following sets of sentences into one sentence. The first sentence has been done for you.**

1. Pizza is cheesy. Pizza is gooey. Pizza is great.

   Pizza is cheesy, gooey, and great.

2. Susan is tall. Susan is skinny. Susan is left-handed.

   _____

3. At camp we play baseball. We jump on trampolines. We go rowing.

   _____

4. Marcia goes to the pool. She swims laps. She practices diving.

   _____

5. Nina won an art contest. She won a game of miniature golf. She won a 50-yard dash.

   _____

   _____

Simple and Compound Sentences

Recall as much as you can about simple and compound sentences. Then turn to handbook page 415 and carefully reread the section on simple and compound sentences.

Example

Simple Sentences: My sister wants to earn money for camp.
She will wash cars for $3.00 each.

Compound Sentence: My sister wants to earn money for camp, so she will wash cars for $3.00 each.

Directions **Think of a time you did something to earn money. Write four simple sentences about your experience. Then combine the sentences so you have two compound sentences. Check the coordinating conjunctions on handbook page 435, and try to use a different one for each sentence. (See page 121 for more on compound sentences.)**

Simple Sentences:

1. _____

2. _____

3. _____

4. _____

Compound Sentences:

1. _____

_____

2. _____

_____

Combining Sentences into Compound Sentences

See handbook page 415 for help with combining sentences by making **compound sentences.**

Example

> *Simple Sentences:* You can go swimming.
> We could take a walk.

> *Compound Sentence:* You can go swimming, or we could take a walk.

Directions Combine each pair of sentences into one compound sentence. Use a comma and coordinating conjunction. The first one has been done for you.

1. I recently made new friends. They are from other countries.

    I recently made new friends, and they are from other countries.

2. Two of them are from Mexico. One is from India.

    _____

3. They have different holidays. We celebrate all of them.

    _____

4. In Mexico, they have Cinco de Mayo. In India, they have Divali.

    _____

    _____

5. I don't speak Spanish or Marathi. My friends speak English.

    _____

The Next Step Write a paragraph or short story about a holiday or custom your family observes. After you've finished, go back and check your sentences. Could any of your short sentences be combined into compound sentences? If so, change them before you exchange stories with a partner and read one another's stories.

_____

_____

_____

_____

_____

_____

_____

_____

_____

_____

_____

_____

_____

Combining Sentences by Using Compound Subjects and Verbs

Another way to combine sentences is to move a subject or verb from one sentence to another. When you do this, you make a **compound subject** or a **compound verb.** (See handbook page 120.)

Examples

Compound Subject: Carl and Suzanne have pet gerbils.

Compound Verb: The gerbils run through a maze and use an exercise wheel.

| **Directions** | Combine each set of sentences below by using a compound subject or a compound verb. The first one has been done for you. |

1. Farrah is a gerbil. Festus is a gerbil, too.

   Farrah and Festus are gerbils.

2. Emily takes care of them. Her mom takes care of them, too.

3. Farrah plays in the bathtub! Festus plays in the bathtub, too!

4. Emily and her mom plug the drain. They put in toys.

5. The gerbils can exercise. They can sleep.

6. But one day Emily's mom made a mistake. She left a bath mat over the edge of the tub.

_____

_____

7. Festus grabbed the mat. He climbed out of the tub! He disappeared!

_____

_____

8. Emily and her mom put Farrah in a cage. They went downstairs.

_____

_____

9. Emily searched for Festus. Her mom searched, too.

_____

10. They found Festus in a heat vent. They rescued him.

_____

11. Festus climbed into a tissue box. He was carried to safety.

_____

The Next Step **Read the whole story of "The Great Gerbil Escape" on page 139 in your handbook. Then imagine that you are Festus! You are telling Farrah all about your adventure. Write some short, choppy sentences telling what you will say to Farrah. Then trade sentences with a partner and try to combine some of each other's sentences. Use any of the different ways you have practiced so far. We have started Festus's story for you.**

"I was bored. I tried to find Emily. I crawled into a hole. It was dark! . . . "

Combining Sentences with Subordinating Conjunctions

One way to combine sentences is to make **complex sentences.** You connect two ideas with a **subordinating conjunction.** (See handbook page 415 for an explanation of complex sentences.)

Example

Many French people settled in Canada *while* people from other parts of Europe settled in the United States.

Directions	Combine the following pairs of sentences to make complex sentences. Be sure to use a subordinating conjunction as explained on handbook page 435.

1. Millions of Jewish people left Russia. They faced prejudice there.

_____

_____

2. People from Great Britain found it easy to adjust to the United States. They already spoke English.

_____

_____

3. Most Irish immigrants came during the 1800s. There was a famine in Ireland.

_____

_____

Directions   Open your handbook to page 110. In the model essay, there are five sentences that have subordinating conjunctions. Copy the sentences below and circle the subordinating conjunctions.

1. _____

_____

_____

2. _____

_____

_____

3. _____

_____

_____

4. _____

_____

_____

5. _____

_____

_____

The Next Step   **Now read each sentence above as if it were two sentences. (Take out the subordinating conjunction.)**

Combining Sentences with Relative Pronouns

One way to combine sentences is to make **complex sentences.** And one way to make complex sentences is with **relative pronouns.** (See handbook pages 121 and 415.)

Example

Danny, *whose* brother is in our class, will bring a present.

Directions	Use the relative pronoun in parentheses to combine each pair of sentences below. The first one has been done for you.

1. My sister Michelle is having a party. Her birthday is today. (**whose**)

My sister Michelle, whose birthday is today, is having a party.

2. These cupcakes are for the party. She made them herself. (**which**)

_____

_____

3. Her best friend is coming. Her friend lives in Brighton. (**who**)

_____

_____

4. I helped put up the decorations. They are in the backyard. (**that**)

_____

_____

Sentence-Combining Review

You've seen how sentence combining can make your writing smoother and more interesting. Now review handbook page 415 and get ready for a challenge!

Rewrite the following paragraphs on the lines below. Combine short, choppy sentences to make smooth ones. Combine them however you choose, as long as the meaning stays the same and your sentences are correct.

There was a barn. It was dusty. It was made of wood. The wood was old. The wood was gray. The nail marks showed signs of rust. There was an old silo. It stood next to the barn. It looked tired. It was every bit as old as the barn.

Just then, Penny appeared. She appeared in front of the barn. The animals looked up at her. They were surprised. Penny never came into the barnyard. Not at this time of day.

Fragments 1

Your handbook explains different kinds of sentence errors and how to correct them. (See page 115.) This activity gives you practice correcting one kind of sentence error: **sentence fragments.**

Examples

Sentence Fragments:

Lives at the zoo. (missing a subject)

The animals in that cage. (missing a verb)

Directions On each line below, put an *S* if the words that follow are a sentence, or an *F* if they are a fragment. For each fragment, figure out what is missing—the subject or the verb—and write that word on the line to the right of the fragment. The first fragment has been marked for you.

_____ **F** _____ **1.** A baby alligator to our science class.   _____ *verb* _____

_____ **2.** Brought it from the zoo.   _____

_____ **3.** It was only about one foot long.   _____

_____ **4.** Named her Alice.   _____

_____ **5.** Was afraid of the alligator.   _____

_____ **6.** Alice afraid of him, too.   _____

_____ **7.** Next week the zookeeper will bring an iguana.   _____

_____ **8.** Our teacher animals.   _____

_____ **9.** Animal visits make our class fun.   _____

_____ **10.** Hope a box turtle comes.   _____

The Next Step Go back to the fragments on page 101 and make them into complete sentences. Add and underline a subject or a verb, whichever is needed. Use correct capitalization and punctuation. The first one has been done for you.

1. _A baby alligator came to our science class._

2. _____

_____

3. _____

_____

4. _____

_____

5. _____

_____

6. _____

_____

7. _____

_____

Fragments 2

This activity gives you some practice correcting sentence fragments.

Examples

Sentence Fragments:

needed help to stand due to polio
(missing a subject)

Roosevelt often in a wheelchair
(missing a verb)

Directions On each line below, put an *S* if the words that follow are a sentence. Put an *F* if they are a fragment. For each fragment, figure out what is missing—the subject or the verb—and write that word on the line to the right of the fragment. The first one has been done for you.

F **1.** Franklin Roosevelt president from 1933 to 1945. _____*verb*_____

_____ **2.** Was elected four times. _____

_____ **3.** He did a lot of other things, too. _____

_____ **4.** Once, he and his friends sailed to an island. _____

_____ **5.** Went there to find buried treasure. _____

_____ **6.** Didn't find any treasure. _____

_____ **7.** Roosevelt something else, though. _____

_____ **8.** Found a nest with four baby birds in it. _____

_____ **9.** He became an avid bird-watcher. _____

_____ **10.** Enjoyed swimming and sailing with his children. _____

_____ **11.** Roosevelt one daughter and five sons. _____

The Next Step Go back to the fragments on page 103 and make them into complete sentences. Add and underline a subject or verb, whichever is needed. Use correct capitalization and punctuation. The first one has been done for you.

1. Franklin Roosevelt <u>was</u> president from 1933 to 1945.

2. _____

    _____

3. _____

    _____

4. _____

    _____

5. _____

    _____

6. _____

    _____

7. _____

    _____

8. _____

    _____

Run-On Sentences 1

Your handbook explains a sentence error called **run-on sentences.** (See page 115.) One way to fix this error is to add end punctuation and a capital letter to split the run-on sentence into two sentences.

Example

Run-On Sentence:
Mark Twain's real name was Samuel Clemens "Mark Twain" was his pen name.

Corrected Sentence:
Mark Twain's real name was Samuel Clemens. "Mark Twain" was his pen name. ▲ ▲

| **Directions** | Correct the run-on sentences below by dividing them into two sentences. Use correct capitalization and end punctuation in your new sentences. If the sentence is not a run-on sentence, put a check mark next to it. The first sentence has been done for you. |

_____ **1.** Mark Twain wrote *Tom Sawyer* and *Huckleberry Finn.* ~~h~~*H*e is

one of America's most famous authors.

_____ **2.** He was born in Missouri he traveled all over the world.

_____ **3.** Before he became a writer, Twain was a riverboat pilot.

_____ **4.** He worked on steamboats on the Mississippi River until

the Civil War started and the river was blockaded.

_____ **5.** Twain was also a silver miner in Nevada he was a

newspaper reporter, too.

_____ **6.** Later, he lived in Hartford, Connecticut, with his wife and

children.

Run-On Sentences 2

A run-on sentence can be corrected by adding a comma and a connecting word to make one correct sentence.

Example

Run-On Sentence:
Grandma Moses lived to be 101 years old she was a centenarian.

Corrected Sentence:
Grandma Moses lived to be 101 years old, *so* she was a centenarian.

Directions **Correct the run-on sentences below by adding a comma and a connecting word (*and, so, but, yet,* etc.). If the sentence is not a run-on sentence, put a check mark next to it. The first one has been done for you.**

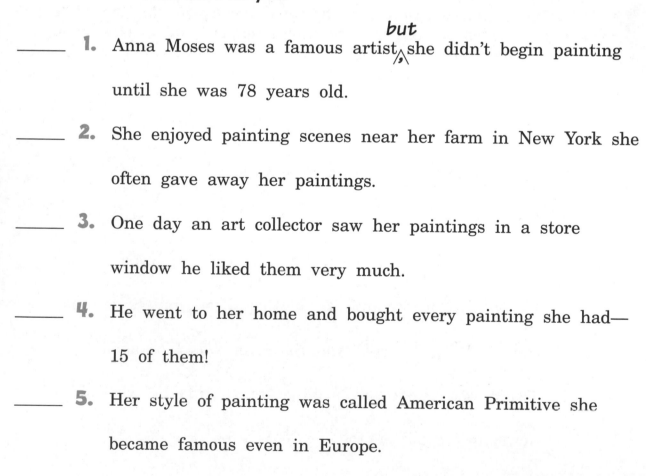

_____ **1.** Anna Moses was a famous artist, *but* she didn't begin painting until she was 78 years old.

_____ **2.** She enjoyed painting scenes near her farm in New York she often gave away her paintings.

_____ **3.** One day an art collector saw her paintings in a store window he liked them very much.

_____ **4.** He went to her home and bought every painting she had— 15 of them!

_____ **5.** Her style of painting was called American Primitive she became famous even in Europe.

Rambling Sentences

Your handbook explains different kinds of sentence errors and how to correct them. (See page 115.) This activity gives you practice correcting one kind of sentence error: **rambling sentences.** A rambling sentence happens when you put too many little sentences together with the word *and*.

Directions   Below are two rambling sentences. Correct them by dividing them into as many sentences as you think are needed. Cross out the extra *and*'s, capitalize the first word of each sentence, and use the correct end punctuation. The first part of number 1 has been done for you.

1. Our class went to the art museum, and a man who worked there
H
gave us a special tour. ~~and~~ He told us about all the artists and
when they lived and he told us that one artist named Vincent
van Gogh cut off his own ear and Raul asked why, and our guide
said that nobody knew for sure and Raul thinks that van Gogh
must have been nuts.

2. Maria's mom owns a restaurant called Old Mexico and it's near
our school and Maria's mom invited our whole class to come to
the restaurant for lunch and our teacher said that we could go,
so we went today and we all got to have anything we wanted,
and almost everybody had two desserts and it was great!

The Next Step You and a classmate each write a rambling sentence. (See how long you can make it!) Then trade and correct each other's rambling sentences.

_____

_____

_____

_____

_____

_____

_____

_____

_____

_____

_____

_____

_____

_____

_____

Sentence Problems

Handbook page 117 explains four common kinds of sentence problems. Review them. Which ones sometimes creep into your sentences?

Examples

Double Subject:
My parents they came here from Australia.
(The pronoun *they* should be omitted.)

Double Negative:
They didn't have nowhere to stay at first.
(Change *nowhere* to *anywhere*.)

> **Directions**   **Most of the following sentences contain sentence problems. Correct them by crossing out or changing the word that is incorrect. If the sentence is correct, put a *C* next to it. The first sentence has been done for you.**

_____ **1.** People who move to the United States from other countries ~~they~~

are called immigrants.

_____ **2.** If there had been no immigrants, there wouldn't be nobody in

the United States except Native Americans.

_____ **3.** The United States was once considered a melting pot, blending

many cultures into one.

_____ **4.** My friend and her father arrived two years ago from India, and

he will be happy to become U.S. citizens.

_____ **5.** Some immigrants who are fleeing from war wish they could of

stayed in their own countries.

_____ **6.** Most of us are either immigrants or descendants of immigrants.

The Next Step Decide which kind of sentence problem is the biggest problem *for you*. Choose a partner, and ask your partner to write a few sentences that contain that sentence problem. Meanwhile, you write a few sentences that contain your partner's biggest sentence problem! Trade papers, and correct each other's sentences.

_____

_____

_____

_____

_____

_____

_____

_____

_____

_____

_____

_____

_____

Sentence Errors Review

In this activity, you will practice correcting different kinds of sentence errors. See "Sentence Errors" on handbook page 115.

Directions	The paragraph below is full of sentence fragments and run-on sentences. Add the needed words and punctuation to make each sentence complete and correct. The first correction has been done for you.

here are

1   You probably know that frogs are amphibians. But∧some

2   additional facts about frogs. Their eardrums are on the outside

3   next to their eyes they can breathe through their skin! Strange

4   creatures. A frog's tongue is attached to its mouth in the front

5   your tongue is attached to the back of your mouth. Is also coated

6   with sticky stuff. Can easily catch insects with it. Most frogs

7   start out as tadpoles some hatch as tiny frogs called froglets.

8   One more fact about frogs. Some frogs estivate that means they

9   bury themselves in sand and stay in a sleeplike state when it is

10 very hot.

Directions	The following paragraph includes many rambling sentences. Correct them by breaking them into shorter sentences.

1   You can watch frogs change from eggs to tadpoles to frogs.

2   All you have to do is go to a quiet pond or creek in the spring

3   and find some frogs' eggs and then bring them home and watch

4   what happens. An adult can help you find them. Make sure you

5   bring home only a few frogs' eggs and cover them in the same

6   water in which you found them and also bring some algae and

7   water plants to use in the water with the eggs. The eggs will

8   become little tadpoles in only about a week and when that

9   happens, you should take most of them back to the pond and

10   keep only one or two and also get some fresh water and plants

11   from the pond. You will see the tadpoles grow back legs first,

12   and then they will grow front legs and their tails will go away,

13   too, and by the way, don't worry if your tadpoles don't eat while

14   they are losing their tails. That's normal. Now your tadpoles are

15   frogs and you should take them back to where you found them

16   when they were only eggs because grown frogs need to eat living

17   insects and they also need to live with other frogs so the frog life

18   cycle can go on.

Changing Sentence Beginnings

When you polish your writing, check how your sentences start. If they all start the same way, your writing will be boring. Read "Change sentence beginnings" on handbook page 65 for ideas.

Directions In the following paragraph, all the sentences start exactly the same way. Using the ideas you found in your handbook, rewrite the paragraph so that most of the sentences have different beginnings. (You can leave one or two the way they are.) The first sentence has been rewritten for you as an example.

Evan leaves a trail of trouble even when he isn't trying. Evan and I were painting pictures at the kitchen table the last time I baby-sat for him. Evan painted a couple of monster faces and then he decided to do something else. Evan offered to help clean up, which surprised me. Evan was carrying the jar of dirty water from our paintbrushes when disaster struck. Evan tripped and the dirty water went flying. Evan gets in trouble even when he tries to help.

Even when Evan isn't trying, he leaves a trail of trouble.

_____

_____

_____

_____

_____

_____

_____

Directions Write about something you did that was amazing, terrific, or funny. Start most or all of your sentences with "I." After you have finished, revise your writing by changing at least three sentence beginnings. Underline the sentences you want to change; then rewrite them at the bottom of this page.

_____

_____

_____

_____

_____

_____

_____

_____

_____

_____

_____

Sentences with changed beginnings:

1. _____

2. _____

3. _____

4. _____

Specific Nouns and Powerful Verbs

Good writing uses **specific nouns** and **powerful verbs.** Handbook page 66 gives examples of both.

Examples

General / Specific Nouns:
Tree/maple; game/hopscotch; dog/Great Dane

Weak / Powerful Verbs:
walk/wander; drink/guzzle; think/ponder

Directions In the sentences below, replace each underlined word with a specific noun or a powerful verb. The first one has been done for you.

       hiked   Split Rock Park

1. We <u>went</u> over to <u>the park</u> Sunday.

2. A <u>man</u> was sleeping under a <u>tree</u>.

3. His <u>drink</u> was next to him.

4. An <u>animal</u> <u>went</u> up and drank out of his cup.

5. Some <u>people</u> were watching and <u>laughing</u>.

6. When the <u>man</u> woke up, a <u>person</u> told him what had happened.

7. Down by the <u>water</u>, some <u>people</u> were feeding the <u>birds</u>.

8. The <u>birds</u> were <u>making noise</u>.

9. We saw a <u>toy</u> floating in the <u>water</u>.

10. Jake said he was going to try to <u>get</u> it.

11. He leaned over and <u>fell</u> into the water.

Directions In the space below, write a few more sentences about the park. Tell what happened next. Make sure to use specific nouns and powerful verbs.

_____

_____

_____

_____

_____

_____

_____

_____

_____

_____

_____

_____

The Next Step **Trade papers with a classmate and read each other's work. Notice the specific nouns and powerful verbs your classmate chose and how they make his or her story different from yours.**

Language Activities

Every activity in this section includes a main practice part in which you learn about or review the different parts of speech. Most of the activities also include helpful handbook references. In addition, The Next Step, which is at the end of most activities, encourages follow-up practice of certain skills.

Nouns

A **noun** names a person, a place, a thing, or an idea. (See handbook page 418.)

Examples

A Person: mom, Bob
A Place: kitchen, Idaho
A Thing: cup, July
An Idea: courage, partnership

Directions Do you ever get mixed-up and say something different from what you mean? Sam Goldwyn used to do that all the time. He was a famous moviemaker when movies were first invented. Below are some things Sam Goldwyn said. Circle all the words used as nouns. The number after each sentence tells you how many nouns it has. The first sentence has been done for you.

1. "The (scene) is dull; tell him to put more (life) into his (dying)." (3)

2. "For your information, I would like to ask a question." (2)

3. "It's spreading like wildflowers!" (1)

4. "You've got to take the bull by the teeth." (2)

5. "This new bomb is dynamite." (2)

6. "When I want your opinion, I'll give it to you." (1)

7. "This book has too much plot and not enough story." (3)

8. "Every director bites the hand that lays the golden egg." (3)

9. "I never put on a pair of shoes until I've worn them five years." (3)

10. "Look how I developed John Hall: He's a better leading man than

    Robert Taylor will ever be—someday." (4; each name counts as 1 noun)

Directions	Below are some more "not quite right" things that different people have said. Again, circle all the words used as nouns.

1. "That guy's out to butter his own nest." (2)

2. "You are out of your rocker." (1)

3. "I'd like to have been an eardropper on the wall." (2)

4. "It's time to swallow the bullet." (2)

5. "We both had haircuts, which made our ears stick out like sore

   thumbs." (3)

6. "I'm sticking my neck out on a limb." (2)

7. "That's a horse of a different feather." (2)

8. "You buttered your bread, now lie in it!" (1)

The Next Step   **Can you figure out what these people meant to say? Choose three of the sentences above; then rewrite them so that they are correct. Circle the nouns in your sentences.**

1. _____

_____

2. _____

_____

3. _____

_____

Common and Proper Nouns

Nouns can be labeled as **common** or **proper.** (See handbook page 418 if you need an explanation of these terms.)

Examples

Common Nouns:
holiday, name, book

Proper Nouns:
Memorial Day, Maria, *Writers Express*

Directions | Underline each word used as a noun in the sentences below; then write *C* above each common noun and *P* above each proper noun. (Notice that the number of nouns is given in parentheses after each sentence.) The first noun has been marked for you.

1   <u>Juan</u> bought a bike from Green's, a hardware store in the

2   neighborhood. *(5)* He bought a secondhand bike, and it seemed to

3   be in very good condition. *(2)* He bought the bike on Saturday,

4   and rode it around on Sunday, but on Monday the handlebars got

5   very loose. *(5)* On Tuesday, he took his bike back to the store

6   and told Mr. Green, the owner, about the handlebars. *(6)*

7   Mr. Green got out his wrench and a couple bolts and fixed the

8   handlebars right away! *(4)* Now Juan thinks his secondhand bike

9   is better than all the new bikes at Green's. *(4)*

The Next Step Look around you and notice all the persons, places, things, and ideas. Then make two lists—one of proper nouns and one of common nouns. See how many nouns you can spot!

Proper Nouns	Common Nouns
_____	_____
_____	_____
_____	_____
_____	_____
_____	_____
_____	_____
_____	_____
_____	_____
_____	_____
_____	_____
_____	_____
_____	_____
_____	_____
_____	_____

Singular and Plural Nouns

A **singular noun** names one person, place, thing, or idea. A **plural noun** names more than one person, place, thing, or idea. (See handbook page 418.)

Examples

 Singular Nouns: sister, dog, car

 Plural Nouns: sisters, dogs, cars

Directions In the following sentences, underline each word used as a noun. (The number of nouns in each sentence is given in parentheses.) Above each noun write *S* if it is singular and *P* if it is plural. The first sentence has been done for you.

1. My little <u>brother</u> eats <u>oatmeal</u> for <u>breakfast</u> every weekday <u>morning</u>. *(4)*
   (S above brother, oatmeal, breakfast, morning)

2. My mom eats cornflakes and toast or muffins. *(4)*

3. She drinks two cups of coffee, too. *(2)*

4. On weekends we have pancakes or waffles and sometimes scrambled eggs. *(4)*

5. Danny eats his pancakes with butter and jam instead of syrup. *(5)*

6. Our grandparents eat a big breakfast every day. *(3)*

7. They make eggs, bacon, fried potatoes, and toast. *(4)*

8. When Danny goes to visit them, they make oatmeal for him. *(2)*

9. He likes brown sugar and milk on his hot oatmeal. *(3)*

10. They give all the leftovers to their cats, Harry and Tom. *(4)*

Directions Write a paragraph about breakfast. Your paragraph could be about

- what you eat for breakfast,
- what you would like to eat for breakfast,
- the weirdest breakfast you can imagine, or
- any other breakfast subject!

_____

_____

_____

_____

_____

_____

_____

_____

_____

_____

_____

_____

The Next Step **When you finish, trade paragraphs with a partner. Underline all the nouns in each other's paragraph. Then label each noun _S_ for singular or _P_ for plural.**

Concrete and Abstract Nouns

Concrete nouns name things that can be touched or seen. **Abstract nouns** name things that cannot be touched or seen. (See handbook page 418.)

Concrete Nouns: flower, shoes, Robert Taylor

Abstract Nouns: information, happiness, decade

Directions Sort the nouns below into concrete and abstract nouns. Write each noun in the correct column. Then add one noun of your own to each list.

question	joy	opinion	thumbs
horse	book	day	liberty
teeth	plot	years	sunshine
dynamite	egg	nest	trust

Concrete Nouns   **Abstract Nouns**

_____   _____

_____   _____

_____   _____

_____   _____

_____   _____

_____   _____

The Next Step **Write three sentences, each using one concrete noun and one abstract noun. An example has been done for you. (You may—but don't have to—use the nouns on the previous page.)**

1. _The boy asked a question._

2. _____

_____

_____

3. _____

_____

_____

4. _____

_____

_____

Uses of Nouns

Nouns can be used in different ways in sentences. You've had lots of practice using **subject nouns,** which are nouns used as the subject of a sentence. But you also need to know how to use **predicate nouns** and **possessive nouns.** (Read about all three uses on handbook page 420.)

Examples

Subject Noun: My <u>sister</u> went to the library.

Predicate Noun: My sister is an <u>artist</u>.

Possessive Noun: My <u>sister's</u> friends like me.

Directions   In the sentences below, label all the underlined nouns. Write an *S* above the noun if it is a subject noun, a *P* if it is a predicate noun, and a *POS* if it is a possessive noun. The first sentence has been done for you.

1. A <u>beagle</u> is a friendly <u>dog</u>.
   <small>S   P</small>

2. The <u>party</u> will be a <u>surprise</u>.

3. <u>Jeremy's</u> <u>cat</u> is a <u>Siamese</u>.

4. <u>Marla's</u> favorite <u>sport</u> is <u>baseball</u>.

5. <u>Jordan</u> became an <u>editor</u>.

6. The <u>winner</u> was <u>Suzanne</u>.

7. <u>Blake</u> knows <u>Lydia's</u> brother.

8. The <u>book's</u> <u>author</u> signed my copy.

9. Our <u>school's</u> track <u>team</u> won the championship.

10. My best hiding <u>place</u> is the <u>attic</u>.

The Next Step **Above each underlined noun, write *S* if it is a subject noun, *P* if it is a predicate noun, and *POS* if it is a possessive noun. (Draw an arrow from each predicate noun to the subject it renames.) The first two have been done for you.**

The Frog's Tail *(a West African folktale)*

            S ⟵——————— *P*

1   In the beginning, Frog was the only animal that didn't have a

2   tail. The other animals teased him. They said Frog was a freak. So

3   Frog begged Nyame, who had made all the animals, to give him a tail.

4   Nyame gave Frog a tail. In return, Nyame said Frog must be

5   Nyame's guard. Frog's job was to guard Nyame's magic well. Nyame

6   told Frog that when it didn't rain for a long time, the other wells

7   would dry up. When that happened, Frog should let all the animals

8   come and drink at Nyame's well.

9   Well, Frog became a bully. Not only did he have a tail, he also

10   had an important job. Soon the rain stopped. All the other wells dried

11   up. The animals came to Nyame's well. But Frog remembered how

12   they had made fun of him, and wouldn't let them drink.

13   When Nyame heard what Frog had done, he took Frog's tail away.

14   Ever since then, young frogs have tails, but they lose them as they

15   grow up.

Nouns as Objects

A noun is a **direct object** when it receives the action of the verb. A noun is an **indirect object** when it names the person to whom or for whom something is done. A noun is an **object of a preposition** when it is part of a prepositional phrase. (See handbook page 420 for more about nouns as objects.)

Examples

Direct Object:	Dennis rides his *bike*.
Indirect Object:	He gave *Wendy* a ride.
Object of a Preposition:	They rode to the *market*.

Directions   **Look at the following sentences and the circled nouns in each. Then label each noun according to which kind of object it is. The first one has been done for you.**

1. Yelena wrote a funny (letter.)   *direct object*

2. Yelena wrote (Mike) a funny letter.   _____

3. Yelena wrote a funny letter to (Mike.)   _____

4. Mom took (me) to the dentist.   _____

5. The teacher wrote on the (chalkboard.)   _____

6. Mr. Marple asked (Rhonda) to mow the lawn.   _____

7. Dr. Fine gave some (medicine) to me.   _____

8. Our dog jumped into the swimming (pool.)   _____

9. Peggy cooked (dinner) for the whole family.   _____

10. Ty drew (Carla) a picture.   _____

| **Directions** | Now write three sentences of your own. Each one should contain a noun used as a different kind of object. Your sentences may contain more than one kind of object. *Special Challenge:* You may want to include compound objects in your sentences, just as you sometimes use compound subjects. Check out this example: |

(object of a preposition)   *(direct object)*

With her new <u>pen</u>, Yelena wrote <u>Mike</u> and <u>Maggie</u> a funny <u>letter</u>.

(compound indirect object)

1. _____

_____

_____

_____

2. _____

_____

_____

_____

3. _____

_____

_____

_____

The Next Step   When you're finished, exchange your work with a classmate. Find and label the nouns used as objects. Did your partner write at least one example of each?

Subject and Object Pronouns

A **pronoun** is a word used in place of a noun. A **subject pronoun** is used as the subject of a sentence. An **object pronoun** is used after an action verb or a preposition. (See handbook page 423.)

Examples

   Subject Pronoun: *I* like movies.

   Object Pronoun: Sheila asked if Bob likes *them*.

Directions   **Each sentence below contains a subject pronoun, an object pronoun, or both. (Some sentences contain three or four pronouns.) Underline and label each subject pronoun *S* and each object pronoun *O*. The first sentence has been done for you.**

1. Sheila and I went to a movie.

2. She liked it, but it was too scary for me.

3. After the movie, Sheila's parents, Mr. and Mrs. Daly, took us to

   a bakery for cupcakes.

4. "You can have any flavor, girls," Mrs. Daly said.

5. "You get a cherry, I will get lemon, and we can share," Sheila said.

6. "Mark is sick," Mrs. Daly said. "We will get a cupcake for him, too."

7. Sheila reminded her that he likes vanilla.

8. "Hey, what about me?" Mr. Daly asked.

9. "No cupcakes for you; you are on a diet!" Mrs. Daly answered.

| Directions | Cross out the subject of each sentence below. Replace the subject with the correct subject pronoun: *he, she, it,* or *they.* The first one has been done for you. |

   She
1. ~~Sheila~~ liked the movie.

2. The movie was scary.

3. After the movie, Mr. and Mrs. Daly picked Sheila and Sue up.

4. Mrs. Daly bought cupcakes.

5. Sheila got a cupcake for Mark.

6. Mark likes vanilla cupcakes.

7. Mark thanked Sheila.

The Next Step All of the sentences above, except one, contain a noun or noun phrase that can be replaced with an object pronoun. (Remember, an object pronoun is used after an action verb or a preposition.) Cross out each noun or noun phrase and write the correct object pronoun (*him, her, it,* or *them*) above it. The first sentence will look like this:

   She   *it*
1. ~~Sheila~~ liked ~~the movie~~.

Possessive Pronouns

A **possessive pronoun** shows ownership. (See handbook page 423.)

Examples

She left *her* purse on the bus.

My cat likes to sit on top of the refrigerator.

When *its* wheels spin, it whistles.

Directions Underline the possessive pronouns in the following sentences. The first sentence has been done for you.

1. Did <u>your</u> mom take <u>our</u> videos back to the store?

2. This book is mine, and that one is hers.

3. Their cat wriggled out of its collar.

4. I will give my book report right after you give yours.

5. Her house is farther from school than our house is.

6. Are these markers yours or his?

7. His cousins like our school better than they like their own.

8. Our team has more players than your team has.

9. Her class has a different lunch hour than my class has.

10. Their school has its own swimming pool.

11. My project will be finished before yours is finished.

Directions   Cross out each underlined word or phrase below, and replace it with the correct possessive pronoun. The first one has been done for you.

1. Tim is taking ~~Tim's~~ *his* dog for a walk.

2. Our teacher showed us pictures of <u>our teacher's</u> vacation.

3. Mohan and Jon won first prize for <u>Mohan and Jon's</u> science project.

4. Whose poem is longer, <u>Philip's</u> or <u>Marie's</u>?

5. The bird is building <u>the bird's</u> nest.

6. The party will be at <u>my family's</u> house.

7. Is this <u>Taylor's</u>?

8. Taylor thought it was <u>Taylor's</u>.

9. The storm left damaged buildings in <u>the storm's</u> wake.

10. Those skates are <u>my skates</u>.

The Next Step   **Write three sentences of your own that correctly use possessive pronouns.**

1. _____

_____

2. _____

_____

3. _____

_____

Indefinite Pronouns

An **indefinite pronoun** refers to people or places that are not named or known. (See handbook page 424 for a list of indefinite pronouns.)

Example

Something special is planned for the party.

| **Directions** | Underline the indefinite pronouns in the following sentences. Some sentences have more than one indefinite pronoun. The first sentence has been done for you. |

1. <u>All</u> of the cookies are gone.

2. Most of the ice cream is gone, too.

3. We need a cowboy hat for the play, but nobody has one.

4. Everybody is studying for the test.

5. Mom said, "Either of you can take the trash out."

6. One of us will have to do it.

7. When we start playing volleyball, anything can happen.

8. All of the players do their best.

9. None of my friends is on my team.

10. The chair got wet because somebody left the window open.

11. We jumped when something made a loud noise downstairs.

12. No one wanted to go and see what it was.

Directions Fill in the seven blanks in the sentences below with any indefinite pronouns that make sense. Then write three sentences of your own using indefinite pronouns.

1. _____ is ringing the doorbell.

2. When it rained, _____ went home.

3. We have _____ we need.

4. Did we forget _____ ?

5. _____ had a great time at the party.

6. _____ went wrong!

7. _____ special happened yesterday.

8. _____

_____

_____

9. _____

_____

_____

10. _____

_____

_____

Person of a Pronoun 1

The **person of a pronoun** indicates the point of view of a story. (Read about "Person of Pronouns" on handbook page 422.) The activities below will help you explore different points of view.

Examples

First-Person Point of View:
I cleaned and scrubbed the cottage all day.

Second-Person Point of View:
You two will go to the ball to meet the prince.

Third-Person Point of View:
She had to leave the ball by midnight.

Directions	Write a different ending to *Cinderella.* Write it from the first-person or third-person point of view. Circle five pronouns in your story. Are most of them in the same person?

_____

_____

_____

_____

_____

_____

The Next Step In a small group, share your story endings and decide which point of view was used in each of them.

Person of a Pronoun 2

Review the lists of personal pronouns on handbook page 421, and also the section on "Person of Pronouns" on page 422.

Examples

First Person: *I* forgot *my* sandwich.

Second Person: *You* can buy *your* lunch.

Third Person: *They* serve great tacos on Fridays.

Directions	In the following sentences, underline the personal pronouns. Above each pronoun, write a 1, 2, or 3 to show whether it is a first-person pronoun, second-person pronoun, or third-person pronoun. The first sentence has been done for you.

1. <u>She</u> likes <u>you</u>, and <u>I</u> like <u>her</u>.
   (3)   (2)   (1)   (3)

2. Do you want to play volleyball with us?

3. I made lemonade, and they built a sand castle.

4. They built a moat around it.

5. Where did you and he go?

6. Do you and she want to come with me?

7. You should ride his bike.

8. They don't know where her car is.

9. He borrowed a bike from her because she wasn't going to use it.

10. You can return it to us or to them.

Pronoun-Antecedent Agreement 1

Antecedent is the name for the noun that a pronoun replaces. The pronouns in your sentences must agree with their antecedents. (See handbook page 421.)

Examples

My *sister* had fun at *her* first clown camp. (The pronoun *her* and the word it replaces, *sister*, are both singular, so they agree.)

Aunt Marietta and *Uncle Bill* enjoy being clowns in parades in *their* city. (The pronoun *their* and the words it replaces, *Aunt Marietta* and *Uncle Bill,* are both plural, so they agree.)

Directions	Circle the pronouns in each of the following sentences. Draw an arrow to each pronoun's antecedent. If a pronoun does not agree with this antecedent, cross it out and write the correct pronoun above it. The first one has been done for you.

1. Kerry and Sydney first got the idea of clowning from ~~her~~ *their* aunt and uncle.

2. Clown camp included local students and adults from around the country, and they lasted all morning every day for one week.

3. Some adults returned to camp because they wanted to learn new tricks.

4. The beginning clowns needed to pick their names.

5. Kerry chose *Peppermint* because they sounds great and tastes good, too.

6. Mom made Kerry's costume of pink polka-dotted material, and she sewed a big plastic hoop in the waist.

7. The curly pink wig and costume made Kerry look like a real circus clown when she wore it.

8. Putting on makeup took a long time for Kerry, and I got to help her.

9. Mom told Kerry, "Sydney can draw a big red smile to match your red rubber nose."

10. The goofy shoes and floppy neck ruffle looked perfect; it added pizzazz to the outfit!

The Next Step **Write an interesting sentence about something unusual that you have done. Exchange sentences with a partner. Then write a second sentence that uses a pronoun in place of one of the nouns in your partner's original sentence.**

_____

_____

_____

_____

_____

_____

_____

_____

_____

Pronoun-Antecedent Agreement 2

An antecedent is the noun that a pronoun replaces. The pronouns in your sentences must agree with their antecedents. (See handbook page 421.)

Examples

Mom said, "*I* want to see Niagara Falls."
(The pronoun *I* and the word it replaces, *Mom*, are both singular, so they agree.)

Josh and *Tim* said *they* wanted to go in the tunnel behind the falls.
(The pronoun *they* and the words it replaces, *Josh* and *Tim,* are both plural, so they agree.)

Directions Write pronouns in the blanks in the following sentences. Be sure each pronoun agrees with its antecedent. Circle the word or words your pronoun replaces. The first one has been done for you.

1. (Mom) and (Dad) said ___*they*___ would like to stay on the Canadian side

   of the falls.

2. After Dad checked into the campground, _____ parked the camper.

3. My brothers and I begged that _____ wanted to go see the falls.

4. Even before we could see Niagara Falls, we could hear _____.

5. As the wide river spilled over and thundered down, _____

   disappeared in clouds of mist.

6. That night, special lighting cast colors on the mist, making _____

   glow like rainbows in the night!

7. We needed rain gear to go in the tunnel because _____ was

very wet.

8. My brothers and I looked funny in the thin yellow raincoats _____

had to wear, but Mom and Dad looked even funnier.

9. As we stood at the lookout behind the wall of water, we were glad to

have the raincoats because _____ protected us from the cold mist.

10. Other people were taking boat tours on *The Maid of the Mist* that

carried _____ right into the mist at the base of the falls.

The Next Step **Write a paragraph about a special place you have visited. When you finish, circle all the pronouns you used. See if you can find the antecedent for each one of them. Sometimes an antecedent is in a previous sentence instead of in the same sentence.**

_____

_____

_____

_____

_____

_____

_____

Types of Verbs

Review the information about verbs on handbook pages 425-426 before you do this activity.

Examples

Action Verb: Most dogs *chase* cats.

Linking Verb: Our dog *is* a bulldog.

Helping Verb: He *could* chase a big cat.

Directions **Read the following sentences and look at the underlined verbs. Decide whether the verbs are action verbs *(A)*, linking verbs *(L)*, or helping verbs *(H)*. Write the correct letter above each. The first one has been done for you.**

                A

1. Rolf, our bulldog, <u>loves</u> doggy biscuits.

2. Those biscuits must <u>taste</u> good, because he <u>hides</u> them everywhere.

3. Then he <u>can</u> <u>snack</u> anytime.

4. I <u>have</u> <u>found</u> biscuits in my shoes.

5. Dad <u>has</u> <u>spotted</u> biscuits under his chewed-up gloves.

6. Rolf <u>chews</u> gloves, too . . . and socks.

7. Oh, yes, and Rolf <u>sneaks</u> cookies, but only the fresh-baked kind.

8. Our family <u>has</u> <u>grown</u> fond of Rolf, though.

9. At least he <u>smells</u> sweet.

10. Rolf always <u>spills</u> my bath powder on his way through the bathroom.

The Next Step Pretend that you have a new pen pal. Write a letter in which you introduce yourself; tell about your life, family, and friends; and ask your pen pal about his or her life. After you finish, go back and underline all the verbs in your letter, and label each one as an action verb *A,* a linking verb *L,* or a helping verb *H.*

Helping Verbs

A **helping verb** comes before the main verb. It helps to describe an action or show the time of the action. (See handbook page 426.)

Examples

We *could have* cut the tree down.

We *will* move the driveway instead.

Directions	In the sentences below, circle each helping verb and underline the verb it helps. (There are three sentences that have two helping verbs.) The first sentence has been done for you.

1. Shaneesha (was) <u>going</u> to the library.

2. She was working on a report about *Mississippi Bridge*.

3. I asked her if she would take my books back.

4. She said I should go to the library, too.

5. "Diana might come, too," Shaneesha said, "so we could all work on our book reports."

6. "That would work well, since I am planning to do mine today."

7. "So, I shall see you there?"

8. "I will ask my mom if it's okay," I answered.

9. Shaneesha said, "If she says you can come, meet us where we were sitting last week."

| **Directions** | Underline the verb in each sentence below. Then rewrite each sentence two times, adding a different helping verb each time. (See handbook page 426 for a list of helping verbs.) An example has been done for you. |

1. Jamie <u>plays</u> the flute.

   Jamie <u>is</u> playing the flute.

   Jamie <u>will</u> play the flute.

2. Tomás helps his little brother.

   _____

   _____

3. Kerry and Jim walk to school.

   _____

   _____

4. We write stories.

   _____

   _____

5. Carlos rides the bus to work.

   _____

   _____

Verb Tenses

The **present tense** of a verb states an action that is happening now, or that happens regularly. The **past tense** of a verb states an action that happened at a specific time in the past. The **future tense** of a verb states an action that will take place sometime in the future. (See handbook page 427.)

Examples

Present Tense:
The cricket, mouse, and cat <u>enjoy</u> talking to one another.

Past Tense:
They <u>pranced</u> about the newsstand half the night.

Future Tense:
The three characters <u>will win</u> the hearts of their readers.

Directions	The three sentences above are about the gentle animals in *The Cricket in Times Square* by George Selden. Now you write some sentences about imaginary animals that you have read about or seen in a cartoon. Write at least two sentences for each of the tenses.

Present Tense: _____

_____

_____

Past Tense: _____

_____

_____

Future Tense: _____

_____

_____

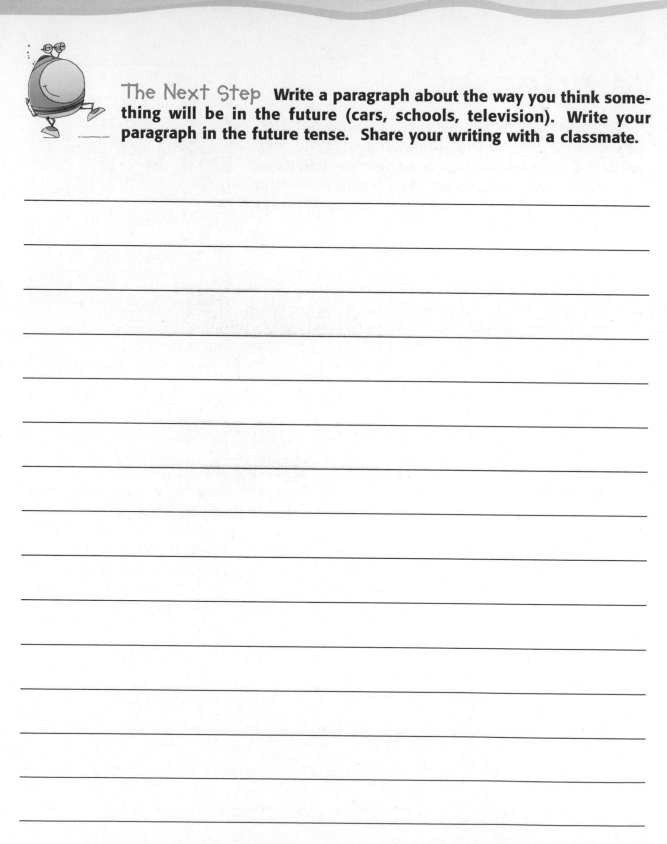

The Next Step **Write a paragraph about the way you think something will be in the future (cars, schools, television). Write your paragraph in the future tense. Share your writing with a classmate.**

Irregular Verbs 1

Irregular verbs don't play by the rules! When you make them past tense, you can't just add "ed" as you do with regular verbs. The only way to learn the past tense and past participles of irregular verbs is to memorize each one. And that takes practice.

Examples

Irregular Verbs: shake, shook, shaken
catch, caught, caught

Directions	Study the chart of irregular verbs on handbook page 429. Then close your book and fill in the missing words in the chart below.

present tense	past tense	past participle
1. blow	_____	(have) *blown*
2. bring	_____	(have) *brought*
3. draw	_____	_____
4. eat	*ate*	_____
5. fly	_____	_____
6. hide	*hid*	_____
7. know	_____	_____
8. lay (to put in place)	_____	_____
9. lie (to recline)	*lay*	_____
10. run	_____	(have) *run*
11. wake	_____	(have) *woken*

The Next Step   Now check your work. Turn to the chart on page 429 and look up each word you filled in. Make a list of all the verbs you got wrong, and write sentences using each one. (If you didn't make any mistakes, choose any two verbs and write a total of six sentences using the principal parts of each verb.)

_____

_____

_____

_____

_____

_____

_____

_____

_____

_____

_____

_____

Irregular Verbs 2

Irregular verbs are not normal! When you change them to past tense or use them with a helping verb, they change in different ways. The only way to know how they change is to learn the different forms of each verb.

Examples

   Irregular Verbs: speak, spoke, spoken
                       fly, flew, flown

Directions Fill in the chart below to see how well you know the different forms for seven common irregular verbs. The first one has been done for you.

Present Tense	Past Tense	Past Participle
see	*saw*	*(have) seen*
	wrote	
drive		
		(have) frozen
	burst	
begin		
		(have) blown
	gave	

The Next Step Now check your work. Turn to the chart on handbook page 429 and look up each word you filled in. List any verbs you got wrong, and write a sentence using each one.

Irregular-Verbs Review 1

This activity is a review of some of the irregular verbs you have practiced.

Directions **Underline the verb in each sentence below. Then rewrite each sentence two times. The first time, change the verb to past tense. The second time, change the verb to the past participle. The first sentence has been done for you.**

1. Mike and Marty <u>bring</u> their turtles to school.

   past tense: _Mike and Marty <u>brought</u> their turtles to school._

   past participle: _Mike and Marty <u>had brought</u> their turtles to school._

2. Schuyler eats a whole box of raisins.

   past tense: _____

   past participle: _____

3. We see our teacher's car.

   past tense: _____

   past participle: _____

4. Amber writes a mystery story.

   past tense: _____

   past participle: _____

5. Our neighbor gives us some homegrown tomatoes.

   past tense: _____

   past participle: _____

_____

Irregular-Verbs Review 2

This activity is a review of some of the irregular verbs you have practiced.

Directions **Write sentences using the past tense and past participle of each verb below. Underline the verbs in your sentences. The first one has been done for you.**

1. know

past tense: _She knew all the questions._

past participle: _She had known all the answers._

2. lay

past tense: _____

past participle: _____

3. lie

past tense: _____

past participle: _____

4. begin

past tense: _____

past participle: _____

5. wake

past tense: _____

past participle: _____

Subject-Verb Agreement 1

One basic rule of writing sentences is that the subject and verb must "agree." (Sentence agreement is explained on handbook pages 116 and 413.)

Examples

My <u>aunt</u> <u>is</u> from Hawaii.
(*Aunt* and *is* agree because they are both singular.)

<u>Native Americans</u> <u>have</u> their own languages.
(*Native Americans* and *have* agree because they are both plural.)

Directions   **Check the following sentences for subject-verb agreement. If the sentence is correct, put a C in front of it. If the subject and verb do not agree, correct the verb. The first one has been done for you.**

_____ **1.** Americans speaks more than 100 different languages.

_____ **2.** Many people moves to the United States from other countries.

_____ **3.** They bring their languages with them.

_____ **4.** Most immigrants comes from Mexico and Vietnam.

_____ **5.** My friend Annie speak Tagalog.

_____ **6.** She is from the Philippines.

_____ **7.** Jorge and Marta speaks Spanish.

_____ **8.** English and Spanish are the most common languages in the

United States.

_____ **9.** Some native-born Americans speak two languages.

Subject-Verb Agreement 2

Subject-verb agreement means that if the subject of a sentence is singular, the verb must be singular, too; if the subject is plural, the verb must be plural. Sometimes you have to read carefully to figure out whether the subject is singular or plural. (See handbook page 116.)

Examples

Megan and Kevin are twins.

Kelly is their sister.

Directions In the sentences below, circle the verbs that agree with the subjects. The first one has been done for you.

1. Every summer the kids in my neighborhood (*put*, *puts*) on a play.

2. Justin and his family (*build, builds*) the stage in their backyard.

3. Isaac or his brother (*is, are*) the director.

4. Charlie and Juanita (*make, makes*) posters and (*sell, sells*) tickets.

5. Carla or her sisters (*is, are*) in charge of costumes.

6. My friend's mom (*help, helps*) with the props.

7. Our parents and my uncle Harry (*provide, provides*) popcorn

   and soda.

8. Usually my friend (*play, plays*) the lead role.

9. The actors and the director (*practice, practices*) all summer.

10. On the last weekend in August, we *(is, are)* finally ready.

11. This year's play, written by Isaac and Sharon, *(is, are)* about

Robin Hood.

12. Jared or Scott *(is, are)* sure to play Robin.

13. The whole neighborhood *(is, are)* waiting for opening night.

The Next Step **Imagine that you and your friends are going to put on a play. Write a paragraph telling who would do all the different jobs. Make sure your subjects and verbs are in agreement.**

_____

_____

_____

_____

_____

_____

_____

_____

_____

_____

Subject-Verb Agreement 3

Making subjects and verbs agree can be harder when the sentence has a **compound subject.** (Review compound subjects on handbook pages 116 and 412.)

Examples

Luke and Leeann listen to CD's.

Mitchell or the twins ride the scooter.

Directions | In some of the following sentences, the subject and verb do not agree. Correct the verbs in those sentences. Put a *C* in front of any correct sentences. The first sentence has been done for you.

_____ **1.** My mother or sisters asks me questions in Spanish.

_____ **2.** Ricki and Rhoda takes me to the movies.

_____ **3.** The teacher or the principal make the announcements.

_____ **4.** The first baseman or the shortstop bat first.

_____ **5.** My brothers and their dog go to the park.

_____ **6.** Rick or his sisters takes the trash out.

_____ **7.** My family and my school recycles paper.

_____ **8.** My mom or my sisters drive me to school.

_____ **9.** My sisters or my mom drive me to school.

The Next Step **On your own paper, using one of the sentences above as a starting point, use as many compound subjects as you can. Be sure that your verbs agree.**

Subject-Verb Agreement Review 1

This activity gives you more practice with subject-verb agreement. (See handbook page 116.)

Directions   Some of the underlined verbs below do not agree with their subjects. If the verb does not agree, cross it out and write in the correct verb. If the verb does agree, put a *C* above it.

1   The students in my class <u>is</u> making an anthology. An anthology

2   <u>is</u> a collection of writings. There <u>is</u> poems, stories, and drawings in our

3   anthology. Every student <u>have</u> one poem or story in the anthology.

4   Lisa and Serena <u>loves</u> to make books. They or our teacher

5   <u>remind</u> us each day what needs to be done next. Don or the Haring

6   twins <u>are</u> designing the front cover. They <u>are</u> the best artists in our

7   class. Tina and Mark, with help from the teacher, <u>is</u> laying out the

8   pages on the computer. Kerry's parents, who own a print shop, <u>is</u>

9   going to print and bind the books. The entire class <u>get</u> to go to their

10   shop to see how they make the books.

11   When the books <u>are</u> ready, all the students in the class <u>gets</u> three

12   copies. There <u>is</u> going to be extra copies to sell, too. We hope we can

13   earn the money we <u>need</u> to pay for the paper and ink.

Subject-Verb Agreement Review 2

Directions   Write about a group project you have done or would like to do. Make sure your subjects and verbs agree.

_____

_____

_____

_____

_____

_____

_____

_____

_____

_____

_____

_____

_____

Adjectives

An **adjective** is a word that describes a noun or a pronoun. Adjectives are used in both the subject and predicate part of the sentence. (See handbook page 430.)

Example

The *expansive* lawn needed mowing.

| Directions | Write four adjectives to describe each mood shown below. |

The Next Step **Let's say you have a dog named Ralphy. Write a name poem, using adjectives to describe him. You may use some of the adjectives above, or think of new ones. (See handbook page 249.)**

R _____

A _____

L _____

P _____

H _____

Y _____

Forms of Adjectives

Turn to handbook page 430 and read about the **comparative** and **superlative** forms of adjectives. Also see the "Irregular Forms" chart on page 431.

Examples

Positive:	Comparative:	Superlative:
smart	smarter	smartest
glorious	more glorious	most glorious

Directions   **In the sentences below, fill in each blank with the correct form of the underlined adjective. The first one has been done for you.**

1. Todd's dog is <u>big</u>, but Samantha's dog is _____*bigger*_____ , and

Charlotte's dog is the _____ dog I've ever seen.

2. Danielle has <u>many</u> relatives, but Paulo has _____ , and Chet

has the _____ relatives.

3. I'm a <u>bad</u> singer, but my mom is _____ than I am, and my

Uncle Roger is the _____ singer I know.

4. Katie is <u>funny</u>, but Marsha is even _____ , and Emily is the

_____ of all the girls in our class.

5. Vanilla ice cream is <u>good</u>, but chocolate is _____ , and

chocolate chocolate-chip ice cream is _____ of all.

6. Summer is a <u>beautiful</u> time of year, but fall is _____ ,

and spring is the _____ of all the seasons.

The Next Step **Write about something that you can do very well. (This is a chance to boast about yourself a little!) Use as many comparative and superlative forms of adjectives as you can, and underline them.**

_____

_____

_____

_____

_____

_____

_____

_____

_____

_____

_____

_____

_____

Colorful Adjectives 1

Colorful adjectives make your writing lively and interesting. When you use exactly the right adjectives to describe something, you give readers a clear, detailed picture of it. Read the paragraph below, noting the colorful adjectives. (Also see handbook page 124.)

Viewed from the <u>hilly</u> terrain of eastern Colorado, the Rocky Mountains have a <u>breathtaking</u> appearance that seems <u>almost</u> <u>unreal</u>. The <u>jagged</u> peaks cut through <u>grey</u>, <u>hovering</u>, clouds, while the <u>snow-covered</u> mountainsides reflect <u>blinding</u> sunshine. The <u>massive</u> formations serve as a wilderness home to <u>golden-brown</u> grizzly bears, <u>sleek</u> mountain lions, and <u>towering</u>, <u>long-legged</u> moose.

| **Directions** | Below are some adjectives that give only a vague picture of what is being described. After each adjective, write three other adjectives that have similar meanings but are more colorful. Use a thesaurus if you need to. An example has been done for you. |

1. large   *gigantic*   *tremendous*   *extensive*

2. small _____ _____ _____

3. quiet _____ _____ _____

4. loud _____ _____ _____

5. old _____ _____ _____

6. nice _____ _____ _____

7. fun _____ _____ _____

8. good _____ _____ _____

Colorful Adjectives 2

Effective adjectives make your writing clearer. (See handbook page 124.)

Example

The *luminous* colors of the fish shone in the *filtered* sunlight undersea.

| Directions | In the following paragraph, replace the underlined words with more colorful adjectives. The first one has been done for you. |

thrilling

1 I started on a ~~fun~~ vacation to Florida with my family. I had

2 never been on such a big plane before. My younger sister and I looked

3 out the windows and laughed at how small everything looked from

4 thousands of feet up in the air. Buildings and fields looked like big

5 patchwork quilts with long roads cutting them into odd patterns. Cars

6 and trucks moved slowly like small bugs. Tall, white, puffy clouds

7 created big canyons right outside our window. Some looked more like

8 the fine mist from a hot shower. Others were like big, flying

9 marshmallows. When the bright sun would hit a river just right, a

10 bright light would explode like a camera flash. We spotted some palm

11 trees. Then the plane began a slow descent. The captain's loud voice

12 announced that we would soon be landing.

Adverbs

Most **adverbs** tell where, how, or when. They describe a verb, an adjective, or another adverb. (See handbook page 432.)

Examples

Where: The car swerved *left* to avoid the pothole.

How: The driver mumbled *loudly*.

When: He would complain to the city *later*.

Directions | In each of the following sentences, circle the adverb and draw an arrow to the word it describes. On the line after the sentence, write whether the adverb tells *where, how,* or *when.* The first sentence has been done for you.

1. Jody and I (often) go to the park. _____ *when* _____

2. Sometimes we play softball. _____

3. We choose our teams carefully. _____

4. We play hard. _____

5. Jody and I always pitch. _____

6. Tasha never misses a pop fly. _____

7. Ira hits the ball hard. _____

8. Most fielders step back for Ira. _____

9. Monica easily catches ground balls. _____

10. Tyrone casually jogs around the bases. _____

Directions	In each of the following sentences, add an adverb that answers the question in parentheses. Write the new sentence on the line. Then circle the adverb and draw a line to the word it describes. The first one has been done for you.

I'm going to the park. *(when)*   I'm going to the park (later.)

Marcia eats.   *(how)*   _____

Rodrigo laughs.   *(how)*   _____

Let's go swimming.   *(when)*   _____

The Next Step Write a personal narrative paragraph about your favorite game, sport, or pastime. Use adverbs to tell when, where, and how. Underline all your adverbs.

_____

_____

_____

_____

_____

_____

_____

_____

_____

Forms of Adverbs

Review handbook page 433. Then complete this activity using the different forms of **adverbs.**

Examples

Positive:	Comparative:	Superlative:
quick	quicker	quickest
softly	more softly	most softly

Directions Rewrite each sentence below. In the first sentence, use the comparative form of the underlined adverb. In the second sentence, use the superlative form of the same adverb. An example has been done for you.

1. Gabriella runs <u>fast</u>.

Gabriella runs <u>faster</u> than Sarah.

Teri runs <u>fastest</u> of all.

2. Bruce played <u>well</u>.

3. Larissa plays her CD's <u>loudly</u>.

4. Terrence reads <u>slowly</u>.

The Next Step **Think of three adverbs that describe how something is done. Then write sentences using the positive, comparative, and superlative forms of each adverb. One has been done for you.**

1. adverb = _carefully_

Jim writes his stories <u>carefully</u>.

Rosa writes hers <u>more carefully</u> than Jim.

Clare writes hers <u>most carefully</u> of all.

2. adverb = _____

_____

_____

_____

3. adverb = _____

_____

_____

_____

4. adverb = _____

_____

_____

_____

Prepositional Phrases 1

Turn to handbook page 434 and review the information about **prepositions** and **prepositional phrases.**

Example

preposition

We have an aquarium in our classroom.

prepositional phrase

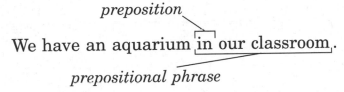

Directions In the sentences below, circle each preposition and underline each prepositional phrase. **The first sentence has been done for you.**

1. Patches ran (around) the room and then jumped (onto) the table.

2. Tom is in his room, hiding under his bed.

3. We went to a restaurant before the play.

4. This book was written by my favorite author.

5. After lunch, we have free time until 1:00.

6. My paper is under that pile of books on the desk.

7. Becky left her skates outside the door and went into the house.

8. She walked through the kitchen toward the stairs.

9. My house is near the corner of Fifth Street and Central Avenue.

10. Go past two stop signs and turn right at Fifth Street.

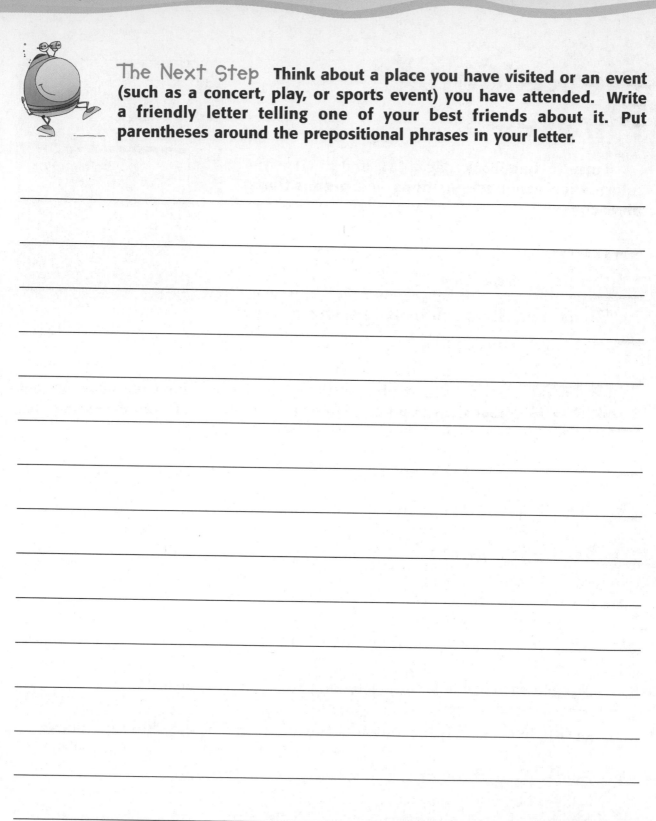

The Next Step Think about a place you have visited or an event (such as a concert, play, or sports event) you have attended. Write a friendly letter telling one of your best friends about it. Put parentheses around the prepositional phrases in your letter.

Prepositional Phrases 2

Turn to handbook page 434 and review the information about **prepositions** and **prepositional phrases.**

Example

preposition

The stream flowed out of Bridge Lake.

prepositional phrase

Directions In the sentences below, write an appropriate preposition in each blank provided and then underline the prepositional phrase. The first one has been done for you.

1   Each summer, my brother Steven and I looked forward to floating

2   _____**down**_____ the stream _____ our grandfather's

3   cabin. We each slipped big black inner tubes _____ our

4   heads and jumped _____ the dock. First we ducked

5   down as we went _____ the wooden bridge. Then we

6   stayed close together as we paddled _____ the cattails

7   and weeds _____ the meandering stream. I liked to

8   have my brother _____ the lead. Once he shouted when

9   he saw a water snake swimming _____ us. Usually,

10   _____ the clear water _____ the fast-

11   moving stream, we watched the schools _____ minnows

12   swimming _____ us. _____ many bends

13   and some shallow spots, we finally came _____

14   our favorite spot—a big culvert going _____ a road.

15   Our yells echoed as we shot through _____ the other

16   side. Then we swirled _____ a churning circle

17   _____ a big, gentle whirlpool.

The Next Step **Write a sentence for each of the prepositional phrases below. Illustrate your favorite sentence.**

1. in the house

_____

_____

2. behind the house

_____

_____

3. throughout the house

_____

_____

4. for the house

_____

_____

Interjections

An **interjection** is a word or phrase used to express strong emotions or surprise. A comma or an exclamation point is used to separate an interjection from the rest of the sentence. (See handbook page 433.)

Examples

Holy cow! That ball is out of here!

Oh, there it is.

| Directions | Pretend you just spent some time with a herpetologist (someone who works with snakes and other reptiles). Write a postcard telling a friend how you felt about being around snakes. Use interjections to let your friend know how strongly you felt about this experience. |

USA ¢

_____, 200 ___

Dear _____,

_____

_____   _____

_____   _____

_____

From,

Conjunctions

Conjunctions are words that connect words, phrases, or clauses. In this activity, you'll practice using all three kinds of conjunctions: coordinating, subordinating, and correlative. (See handbook page 435.)

Examples

Coordinating Conjunction: Joe wanted to come, *but* he had a cold.

Subordinating Conjunction: He can come with us *when* he is better.

Correlative Conjunctions: *Neither* Joe *nor* his sisters feel like shopping.

Directions Connect each group of words below to make one sentence, using a conjunction or a set of correlative conjunctions. In parentheses, indicate which of the three kinds of conjunctions you have used. The first one has been done for you.

1. Sue brought treats to class. Sue brought soda to class.

   Sue brought treats and soda to class. (coordinating conjunction)

2. Jason got the flu. He played football in the rain.

   _____

   _____

3. Our teacher may lead the assembly. Our principal may lead the assembly.

   _____

   _____

4. Yelena got a new haircut. She doesn't like it.

   _____

   _____

Coordinating Conjunctions

Coordinating conjunctions connect equal parts. For example, coordinating conjunctions can connect two words, two phrases, or two clauses. (See handbook page 435.)

Example

My cookie jar is full, *but* it is full of dog biscuits.

Directions Use one of the following coordinating conjunctions to fill in the blank in each sentence below.

| and | but | or | so | yet |

1. My dog Harold is small _____ strong.

2. He has white paws _____ shaggy ears.

3. All afternoon he sleeps on the porch _____ in the house.

4. When I get home, he wants to run _____ play.

5. Harold is fat _____ fast.

6. He chases squirrels _____ our cat.

7. Harold is seven years old _____ still plays like a puppy.

8. He growls at the neighbor's German shepherd _____ hides when he hears thunder.

9. Harold likes to swim in the lake, _____ he doesn't like being out in the rain.

Directions Use a comma plus a coordinating conjunction from the list on page 169 to connect each pair of simple sentences below.

1. Harold loves dog food. He loves people food, too.

   _____

   _____

2. I give Harold cookies. He's always happy to see me.

   _____

   _____

3. He likes hamburgers. He's not supposed to have them.

   _____

   _____

4. Harold loves bones. He looks for them in grocery bags.

   _____

   _____

5. Harold likes to swim in the lake. He chases the Canadian geese.

   _____

   _____

6. Harold barks at our cat. He never barks at strangers.

   _____

   _____

Subordinating Conjunctions

Use a **subordinating conjunction** to connect two clauses to make a complex sentence. (See handbook page 435.)

HURRAY!

Example

We didn't have time to go fishing *although* we had poles and bait.

Directions Choose subordinating conjunctions from the following list and write them on the lines to complete the story.

> after, although, as if, because, before, if, in order that, since, so, that, though, unless, until, when, where, while

1 We were in art class _____ our principal reminded

2 everyone that the dress rehearsal before the concert would begin at

3 6:00 p.m., sharp! _____ Matt arrived just five minutes

4 before the concert, Mr. Martin, the choir director, told him that he

5 would have to miss out on the party. _____ the concert

6 was over, Matt raced off the bleachers and disappeared. We spotted

7 him using the office phone. We were surprised to see Matt at the

8 party later _____ he explained his reason for being late.

9 _____ he was still announcing his new brother had just

10 been born, we started clapping. _____ he knew he had a

11 new brother, he still didn't know the baby's name.

The Next Step Write your own school-related story, using subordinating conjunctions to make at least three complex sentences. Then exchange stories with a classmate and circle the complex sentences in his or her story.

Conjunctions Review

This activity is a review of coordinating and subordinating conjunctions. (See handbook page 435.)

Directions   **Each sentence below has one coordinating conjunction and one subordinating conjunction. Underline both, and write _C_ above each coordinating conjunction and _S_ above each subordinating conjunction. The first sentence has been done for you.**

1.   Let's shoot baskets <u>or</u> play catch <u>until</u> it gets dark.

2.   While it is snowing, we can make a snowman and a snow fort.

3.   The new boy doesn't know us, but he'll come to our party if we invite

    him.

4.   My mom and I like to watch videos when it's rainy.

5.   When our teacher is sick, Mr. Diaz or another substitute comes to our

    class.

6.   Tina does her homework and her chores before she eats dinner.

7.   We heard the kitten mewing, yet we couldn't tell if the sound was

    coming from the closet.

8.   Juan and I walked home after we watched the fireworks.

9.   Terri wants to come over, but she can't come unless she gets over

    her cold.

10.   Because it is snowing, school may be canceled or delayed.

Directions   Add the needed conjunctions to the sentences below.   Then write three sentences of your own, using conjunctions and underlining them.

1. _____ our parents aren't home, Jan _____ I are making

dinner.

2. Jared _____ my sister walks the dog _____ we leave for

school.

3. It's Monday, _____ there is no school _____ it's a

holiday.

4. _____ the thunderstorm, the sun came out, _____ the

air was still cold, _____ it was windy.

5. _____

_____

_____

6. _____

_____

_____

7. _____

_____

_____

Parts of Speech Review 1

This activity is a review of all the parts of speech you have studied.

| **Directions** | Below is a fable from Aesop. Above each underlined word, write what part of speech the word is. The first two have been done for you. |

The Crow and the Pitcher

1   Once there was a <u>crow</u> *[noun]* who was so thirsty he couldn't <u>speak</u> *[verb]*. He

2   found a <u>large</u> pitcher of water <u>in</u> a garden. He <u>lowered</u> his beak into

3   the pitcher to drink. <u>But</u> there was only a little <u>water</u> in the pitcher,

4   and he couldn't reach it. <u>He</u> thought of breaking the pitcher, but <u>it</u>

5   was too <u>strong</u>. He tried <u>hard</u> to turn the pitcher over, but it was too

6   heavy. The <u>poor</u> crow was about to give up <u>when</u> he <u>noticed</u> some

7   pebbles in the garden. This gave him a wonderful idea. "<u>Yes!</u>" he

8   thought to himself. "I will have a drink after all!" He <u>quickly</u> picked

9   up a pebble in his <u>beak</u> and dropped it <u>into</u> the pitcher. As he did this

10   again <u>and</u> again, the water rose <u>higher</u> and higher in the pitcher.

11   Finally the crow was able to reach the water and drink.

Directions Open your handbook to the sample story "Amanda Stands Tall" on page 225. List four different words from the story for each part of speech. (You will find only three interjections.)

Nouns

_____

_____

_____

_____

Verbs

_____

_____

_____

_____

Pronouns

_____

_____

_____

_____

Adverbs

_____

_____

_____

_____

Adjectives

_____

_____

_____

_____

Prepositions

_____

_____

_____

_____

Interjections

_____

_____

_____

Conjunctions

_____

_____

_____

_____

Parts of Speech Review 2

Directions   Write the part of speech for each list of words on the line in the circle. See handbook page 417 for a list of the eight parts of speech.

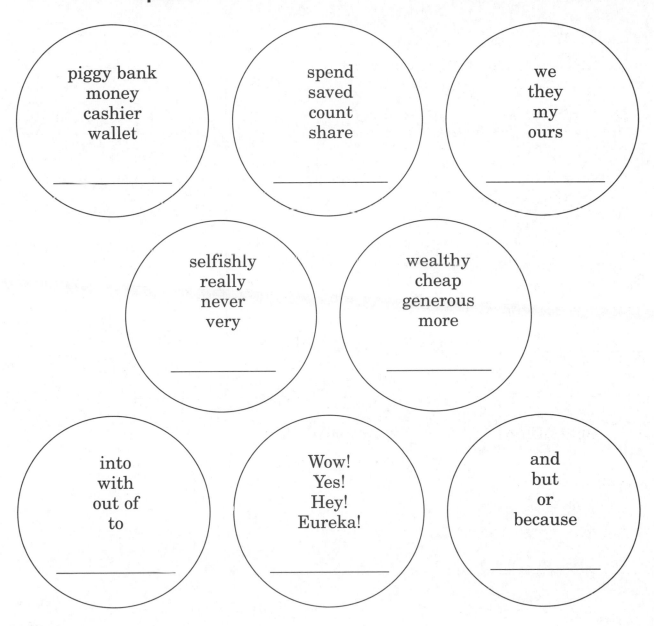

piggy bank
money
cashier
wallet

_____

spend
saved
count
share

_____

we
they
my
ours

_____

selfishly
really
never
very

_____

wealthy
cheap
generous
more

_____

into
with
out of
to

_____

Wow!
Yes!
Hey!
Eureka!

_____

and
but
or
because

_____

The Next Step   **Now write a sentence using as many of the parts of speech as you can. Use some of the words in the circles.**